HISTORY OF THE GUN
— IN —
500
PHOTOGRAPHS

Contents

The earliest weapons were defined by human strength and ingenuity. Then came the discovery, possibly in 10th-century China, that combining charcoal, potassium nitrate, and sulfur could cause explosions.

Innovative gunsmiths introduced features that made it easier for a single shooter to aim, fire, and hit a target. The new matchlock ignition device would remain popular through the early 1700s.

More sophisticated ignition devices led to weapons that were smaller and easier to carry. That meant they could also be concealed, introducing fears about guns and crime.

The early settlers mostly relied on basic matchlocks brought from the Old World. But by the 18th century, American gunsmiths were producing flintlocks the colonists could call their own.

Early 19th-century gunsmiths fitted pistols, muskets, carbines, and rilfes with percussion caps, which allowed weapons to be fired more rapidly and reliably in most any kind of weather.

In 1910, Sir Hiram Maxim, inventor of the first fully automatic machinegun, showed the weapon to his grandson.

Introduction

The past and present of firearms converge in the tiny southern Austrian town of Ferlach, just north of the Slovenian border. Gunsmiths there have crafted weapons since the 1550s, when Ferdinand I, emperor of the Holy Roman Empire, paid Belgian artisans to form a guild to take advantage of Ferlach's iron deposits and water supply. Ferdinand worried about more than hunting game; he feared the Ottomans and needed high-quality arms.

Today, the Ferlach tradition of hand-making guns continues in the atelier of gunsmiths such as Peter Hofer, whose wares are favored by the globe's elite. With eight assistants, who work on only 20 bespoke weapons at a time, the Hofer shop produces such wonders as the Hummingbird, a side-by-side rifle chambered for tiny .17-caliber rounds to hunt birds or small game. The walnut burl stock comes from an 800-year-old Turkish tree; gold-and-enamel birds flit against a backdrop of engraved-steel flowers. Depending on the details, prices begin at $250,000 and can exceed half a million dollars.

Around a few bends of Ferlach's narrow streets, an altogether different sort of firearm is manufactured. Taking advantage of the same local craftsmen's tradition, the international pistol maker Glock GmbH runs a components factory. Sold worldwide for a retail price beginning at about $600, the Glock semiautomatic large-capacity handgun offers blunt efficiency. It's favored by law enforcement and millions of civilians, especially in the United States, where Glock has led a move away from wooden-and-steel revolvers like the Colt and Smith & Wesson toward the plastic black-matte-finish pistols now carried by two thirds of American police.

History of the Gun in 500 Photographs tells the fascinating story of how weapon technology evolved from the earliest cannon to more portable firearms to the advances of gunmakers like Samuel Colt, John Browning, Hiram Maxim, John Garand, Mikhail Kalashnikov, and Gaston Glock. It starts in the premodern age of swords and bow and arrow, when inventors experimented with mixtures that would eventually produce explosive powder. That powder in turn would propel projectiles through a barrel, travelling far beyond the reach of a man with a blade or spear, to fell foes (or dinner) at a great distance.

Bringing the story to life are stunning images and photographs allowing readers to experience the evolution up close, starting with changes to ignition systems, from the matchlock to the wheellock and its successor, the flintlock. The book traces the rise of sporting and hunting guns and how they led to the creation of pistols and revolvers and in time, repeat-firing and fully-automatic weapons. Of course, *History of the Gun in 500 Photographs* is not just the story of firearms as objects: It is a tale of how technology, politics, and warfare have intertwined over the centuries and the lethal role guns have played in conquering new lands, in the defense of ideals, and in quotidian civilian life. To that end, there are also images to illustrate guns being used on the battlefield, starting with artwork of the Hundred Years' War through photographs of the Civil War and the deadly conflicts of the 20th and 21st centuries.

The history of the gun and the history of global culture clearly are interconnected. Since the first firearms appeared in the Middle Ages, new developments have reflected successive waves of human needs and ingenuity. *History of the Gun in 500 Photographs* is a visual record of these critical tools, the people who designed and used them, and the impact they've had on our world.

1 | BLACK POWDER, ALCHEMY, AND BOMBARDS

THE EARLIEST WEAPONS WERE DEFINED BY HUMAN STRENGTH AND INGENUITY.
THEN CAME THE DISCOVERY OF A HISTORY-CHANGING CHEMICAL REACTION.

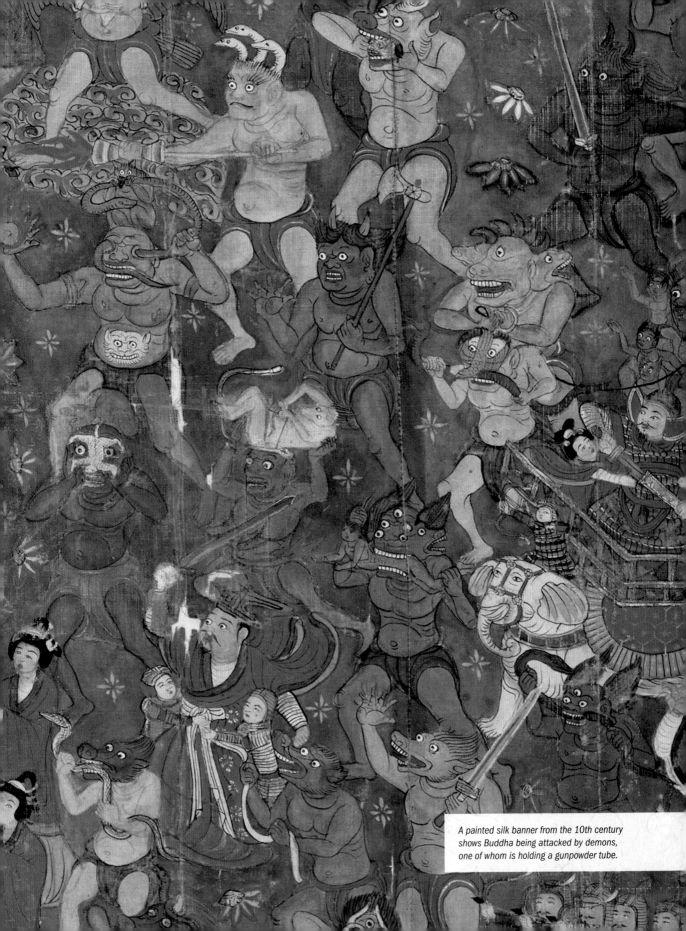

A painted silk banner from the 10th century shows Buddha being attacked by demons, one of whom is holding a gunpowder tube.

An Explosive Power

THE EXACT ORIGINS OF GUNPOWDER ARE UNCLEAR. BUT EARLY TAOIST
TEXTS REFER TO INCENDIARY POTIONS CREATED BY ALCHEMIST MONKS.

The story of firearms begins with chemistry: the invention of gunpowder.

For millennia men expressed hostility by hurling hard objects at each other and stabbing foes with sharpened sticks. Ancient armies besieged enemy castles by harnessing mechanical ingenuity. They launched waves of flaming arrows, enormous stones, rotting animal carcasses, and even stinking loads of excrement.

But the discovery, possibly in 10th-century China, that combining charcoal, potassium nitrate (or saltpeter), and sulfur could cause explosions and, if properly channeled, send matter flying with deadly effect, changed the course of conflict.

Alchemists Searching for Immortality

The exact timeline of the development of "black powder" is unclear. But Taoist texts from the ninth and 10th centuries include references to the incendiary properties of potions created by alchemist monks. Some sustained burns and there was at least one report of a workshop going up in flames. For the monks, it was a hazard of searching for an elixir yielding immortality. For

some of the holy men's contemporaries, however, the black powder may have suggested a way of limiting mortality, rather than extending it. It is believed that Chinese of the era had the idea to use black powder in rudimentary bombs, grenades, and land mines against invading Mongols. The Mongols, in turn, are thought to have carried knowledge of black powder across Asia, spreading it through the Middle East and on to Europe.

In 1241, for example, advancing Mongol forces used powder-powered weapons to help trounce defenders of the Kingdom of Hungary and lay waste to their villages during the Battle of Mohi. Ideas moved from East to West, and soon intermingled with European innovations. The 13th-century writings of English philosopher and Franciscan monk Roger Bacon contain cryptic references to exploding powder, while medieval alchemists across the continent began to experiment with elements of black powder in their attempts to "transmute" lead to gold.

Part of the fascination with these evolving weapons were their terrifying dramatics. Not only did the arms have the capacity to knock down and kill opponents at great

THE MYSTERIOUS FRIAR BACON

In the 19th and early 20th centuries, certain historians identified Roger Bacon (1241–1292) as a major figure in the development of firearms. Some researchers asserted that the Franciscan friar's writings contain a cryptogram describing the ratio of ingredients needed for gunpowder. This view of Bacon fit with a broader impression that he was an early scientist of mystical bent.

While it's possible that Bacon saw a demonstration of Chinese firecrackers, modern historians now doubt that he understood the concept of storing and releasing explosive energy via gunpowder. The passages in question probably did not originate with Bacon, and in any event the mixture described has the wrong proportions of ingredients to power a firearm.

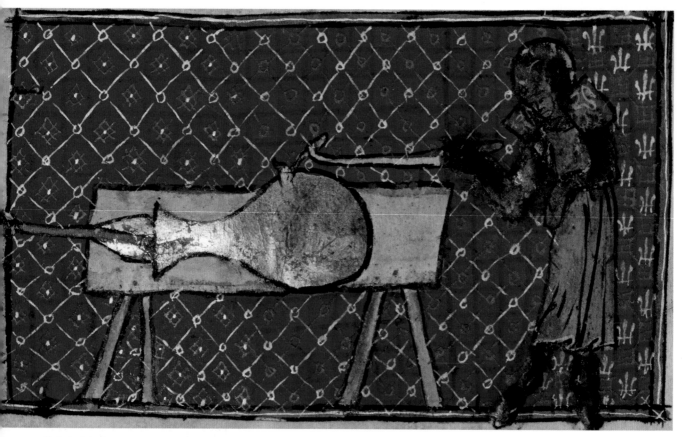

Early Look *In his treatise on siege weapons, 14th-century English scholar Walter de Milemete included what might be the first illustration of a firearm. The weapon, called a pot-de-feu, was a primitive cannon made of iron.*

distances, their repeated explosions generated impressive noise, flames, and smoke. The armored knight on a grand steed suddenly had to both carefully watch his back and negotiate threatening new conditions out on the battlefield.

The Birth of the Cannon

By the late 13th century, military inventors realized they could use black powder to fire projectiles from an iron tube closed at one end. The cannon (from the Latin *canna*, referring to the hollow stem of a reed) was

The chemical instability of early gunpowder recipes led to unintended explosions. Crude metallurgy meant cannon frequently burst apart.

born. The closed end of the weapon came to be known as the breech. Powder and then a projectile were loaded via the open end, or muzzle. A soldier ignited the powder with a torch or smoldering ember through a touchhole in the rear. Rapidly expanded gases from the explosion propelled the ammunition from the barrel—the same basic principle used in firearms to this day.

Illuminated manuscripts of the era show soldiers igniting vase-shaped weapons firing arrow-shaped projectiles. Other early

Battle of Crecy *An illuminated manuscript by medieval French author Jean Froissart included this image of the Battle of Crecy (1346), during the Hundred Years' War. Cannon may have been used in the struggle, but the decisive weapons were the bow, axe, mace, dagger, and sword.*

FIREARMS ON THE BATTLEFIELD

Mongol warriors are thought to have carried knowledge of black powder from China, through the Middle East, and on to Europe.

800-900 While searching for elixirs for a longer life, Taoist monks discovered explosive black powder.

1241 Europeans encountered black powder, brought by Mongols from China, in a battle against the Mongol Empire.

1260 Muslim soldiers packed early cannon with black powder in their conflict with Mongols at the Battle of Ain Jalut.

1346 British forces fighting the French during the Hundred Years' War may have used bombards, an early form of artillery, at the Battle of Crecy.

1453 The arsenal used by Ottoman Turks to capture Constantinople included wheeled cannon. The conquest marked the end of the Roman Empire.

1476 During the Battle of Morat, in which the Swiss faced off against Burgundy, both sides wielded hand cannon.

900
1000
1100
1200
1300
1400
1500

cannon propelled carved stones and iron balls to assault castle walls. England's King Edward III used a type of cannon called a bombard against the Scots in the 1320s, and there are reports that cannon were used in the Hundred Years' War.

Exploding Cannon

Primitive artillery did not always operate effectively. The chemical instability of early gunpowder recipes led to unintended explosions. Crude metallurgy meant that cannon frequently burst apart. Even when they worked properly, early muzzle-loaded weapons weren't terribly accurate, and increasingly sophisticated fortifications limited their impact.

Yet the psychological and physical effects of detonation changed the nature of warfare, allowing armies that deployed cannon in numbers to prevail against entrenched targets. By the 15th century, French and Italian artillery makers were producing transportable wheeled cannon used by such rulers as King Louis XI of France and his successor, Charles VIII, to consolidate power.

Early Cannon and Artillery

MILITARY DESIGNERS BEGAN TO CREATE CANNON THAT COULD FIRE
ARROW-SHAPED ITEMS, CARVED STONES, IRON BALLS, AND MORE.

As black powder was adopted to fire projectiles, weapon design began to evolve. Metal forgers worked with iron and bronze to create weaponry that varied greatly in caliber, mobility, range of fire, angle of fire, and firepower. Early cannon were loaded at the muzzle and ignited with a smoldering matchcord or a red-hot poker.

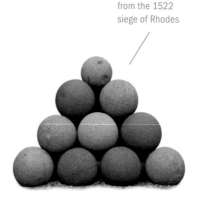

Cannonballs from the 1522 siege of Rhodes

▶ **DARDANELLES GUN**

Country:	Turkey
Date:	1464
Length:	17ft
Bore:	25in

This 18-ton bronze bombard was constructed in two parts (the rear powder chamber is shown at right), and its projectiles could smash fortress walls a mile away.

▶ **16TH-CENTURY BRONZE GUN**

Country:	Germany
Date:	1570
Length:	5ft 10in
Bore:	1.6in

This gun was embossed with a warning: "Who tastes my eggs won't find them pleasant."

Two side-mounted pegs facilitated wheeled transport.

◀ **15TH-CENTURY BRONZE CANNON**

Country:	France
Date:	1478
Length:	7ft 3in
Bore:	9.6in

This 1.6-ton bronze cannon, a technological leap over its iron-forged predecessors, likely required ten times its weight in charcoal to melt the bronze.

The breech could hold up to 150 pounds of powder.

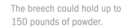

The barrel is crowned by an intimidating monster head.

◄ 15TH-CENTURY BOMBARDS

Country: Great Britain

Date: circa 1430

Material: wrought iron

In 1434, during the Hundred Years' War, the British army abandoned these twin bombards on the coast of France.

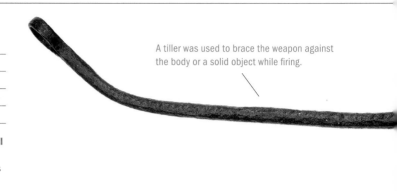

A tiller was used to brace the weapon against the body or a solid object while firing.

▶ IRON HACKBUT

Origin: Netherlands

Date: circa 1500

Barrel Length: 28in

Caliber: .90

Made entirely of iron with a small touchhole, this 12-pound, four-foot hackbut, or "hook gun," was mainly used by foot soldiers.

Enter the *Hand Gonne*

PORTABLE FIREARMS WERE A BIG STEP FORWARD ON THE BATTLEFIELD, BUT IT OFTEN TOOK TWO SOLDIERS TO FIRE THEM.

Parallel with the spread of cannon technology came the invention of portable muzzle-loaded firearms suitable for use by individual infantrymen.

This miniaturization of gunpowder weapons led to the widespread introduction in the 15th century of "hand cannon," also known as *hand gonnes*. Soldiers held these crude forerunners of modern firearms under the arm or braced against a shoulder. Some early models, heavy and ungainly, had to be steadied on a stake and required two men to aim and fire. The user ignited the powder by means of a smoldering length of cord, or "slow match," susceptible in wet weather to becoming soggy and unusable.

By contemporary standards, the one-man 15th-century French hand gonne barely resembled a firearm at all. It consisted of just a small, smoothbore iron barrel one inch or so in diameter attached to a flat wooden stock by means of thick iron bands. Soon, though, hand cannon assumed the rough shape of a modern pistol, with a grip that bent downward from the barrel at roughly a 30-degree angle. Both the Swiss Confederate Army and their opponents, the soldiers of French ruler Charles the Bold, used such pistols during the Battle of Morat (1476). By the 16th century, craftsmen in Spain and elsewhere were fashioning hand cannon from bronze and decorating them with animal imagery and other flourishes. For those who could afford it, the firearm became a work of art.

The Force of the Arquebus

The earliest weapon vaguely resembling a modern long gun—a firearm with a wooden stock and extended barrel—was known as the arquebus and appeared in the early 1400s. The weapon was also known as a harquebus, harkbus, or hackbut,

▲ 15TH-CENTURY ARQUEBUS

Origin:	Europe
Date:	1470–1500
Barrel Length:	40in
Caliber:	1.2

Columbus conquered the New World with similar weaponry.

An iron barrel supported by a strong wooden stock was a significant step toward modern gunmaking.

from the Dutch *haakbus,* meaning "hook gun."

Typically, an arquebus was muzzle-loaded by a soldier who packed it with powder and a lead ball, then ignited the powder by means of a handheld matchcord—an approach that did not solve the difficulty of shooting in damp conditions. It had an iron smoothbore barrel of perhaps 40 inches in length that was connected to a wooden stave (a narrow block) that the soldier would clamp under his armpit to stabilize the weapon as he fired it. (In time, the stave, designed for greater comfort and ease of use, evolved into the familiar wooden shoulder stock.)

Arquebuses achieved impressive force and penetration. Modern-day experiments with replicas have shown that when they worked, the weapons could hurl an iron ball that pierces steel 1.5 millimeters thick. On the downside, they were inaccurate, a problem designers attempted to solve by including a hook near the mouth of the barrel to place over a wall or other stable object.

By the 16th century, gun designers had improved firing systems so that the arquebus and its successor, the musket, were easier to handle and somewhat more reliable.

右引大毬以紙為毬内實埠石肩可重三五斤整黄爉
渥青炭末為泥周堼其物貫以麻繩凡将放火毬凡
先敷此毬以導遠近
一丈二尺外以紙井雜藥傅之又施鐵錐路透令焰出
有逆習放時燒鐵錐烙透令焰出
藜藜大毬以三枝六首鐵刀以藥圓之中貫麻繩長
火桒法用硫黄
一斤四兩焰硝二斤半寫炭末五兩渥青二兩半乾
漆二兩半擣為末竹指一兩一分麻指一兩一分旬

Just Add Sulfur

It took early experimenters many centuries to perfect recipes for effective gunpowder consisting of sulfur and charcoal, both fuels, and saltpeter, an oxidizer. An 11th-century Chinese text, Wu Ching Tsung Yao (Complete Essentials from the Military Classics), refers to mixtures used in firecrackers, as well as rudimentary flamethrowers and rockets. The formulae, scholars determined, allowed for incendiary effects—the ignition of flame—but not the gas-releasing explosions needed to propel a projectile. The problem? Insufficient saltpeter.

Hand Cannon

THESE WEAPONS WERE CRUDE FORERUNNERS
TO MODERN FIREARMS.

Over time, simple hand cannon evolved into harquebuses—muzzle-loaders with an underside hook that could be used to steady the weapon on a wall or portable support. Some also featured a wooden shoulder stock that functioned as a brace. Echoes of this design element can be seen in the modern gun stock.

The "tail" functioned as a handle.

▼ MEDIEVAL HAND CANNON

Origin: Europe

Date: circa 1350

For ammunition, fighters often packed this hand-forged gun with stones and nails.

Excavated from the grounds of a German castle

▲ BRONZE HAND CANNON

Country: China

Date: 1424

Length: 14 1/16in

Caliber: .59

This hand cannon is on display at New York's Metropolitan Museum.

Powder Magic *A hot iron rod placed in the touchhole ignited the powder to loudly propel projectiles.*

◄ HAND CANNON

Origin: Europe

Date: late 15th century

Barrel Length: 7 1/4in

Bore: .625

This band-reinforced cast iron gun weighed only 1 1/8 pounds.

Barrel ends with slightly flared muzzle

◄ FIRE STICK

Origin: Western Europe

Date: circa 1380

Barrel Length: 6in

Caliber: .78

To use the fire stick, also called a Bâton à feu, a soldier inserted a wooden pole into the breech.

► METAL HAND GUN

Origin: China and Korea

Date: 17th century

This three-barrel gun was often used as a signaling device, but it may also have been used on the battlefield.

2 | MATCHLOCKS AND MUSKETS

INNOVATIVE GUNSMITHS INTRODUCED FEATURES THAT MADE IT
EASIER FOR A SINGLE SHOOTER TO AIM, FIRE, AND HIT A TARGET.

Englishmen with muskets battle with Hawaiian Islanders in an engraving showing the death of the Royal Navy's Captain James Cook.

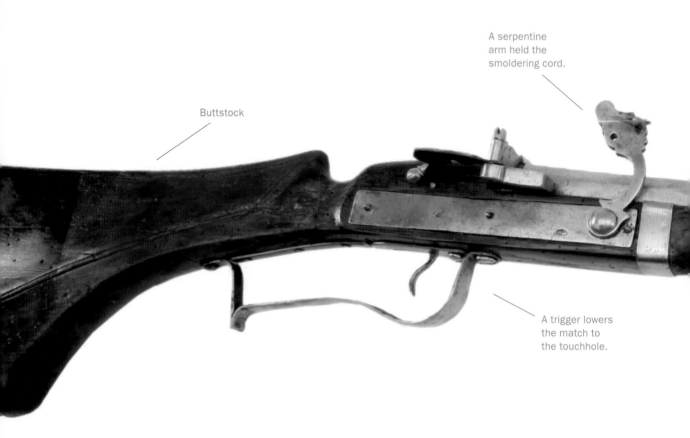

A serpentine arm held the smoldering cord.

Buttstock

A trigger lowers the match to the touchhole.

Building a Better Firearm

GUNSMITHS IN EUROPE AND ASIA SEARCHED FOR NEW WAYS TO IGNITE BLACK POWDER, TO MAKE WEAPONS EASIER FOR SOLDIERS TO USE, AND TO INCREASE ACCURACY.

The proliferation of military and sporting firearms in Europe, Asia, and elsewhere gave rise to a new class of craftsmen whose designs and ambitions drove the advancement of small arms. These gunsmiths searched for more reliable means of igniting powder, more potent formulations of the powder itself, and ways to make guns easier for a single man to use. Ultimately, designers aimed for weapons that allowed for repeated shots without reloading and, of course, they yearned to improve accuracy. The next critical chapter in the story of firearms involves the development of the matchlock firing system.

A Slow Burn

Until about the 16th century, soldiers set off the powder charge for a hand cannon or arquebus by lighting a short length of cord soaked at one end in a chemical, often potassium nitrate (saltpeter), to slow the burning process. The procedure was decidedly awkward: It required the gunman

▼ EARLY 16TH-CENTURY MARTIAL
MATCHLOCK MUSKET

Country: Spain

Date: circa 1530

Barrel Type: smoothbore

In 1565, Spain used matchlocks to establish
St. Augustine, Florida, the first permanent
European settlement in what would become the
United States. This gun was designed to be used
with a forked rest.

FULL VIEW

This musket was
muzzle loaded.

to balance a heavy weapon while
bringing the "slow match" into contact
with the gun's small touchhole. Then
the flame leapt through the opening
and lit the powder.

The introduction of the matchlock
gun made ignition easier, if not
exactly a snap. This new generation of
weapons were still muzzle-loaded by
means of a slender wooden "ramrod"
used to force powder and a ball down
through the barrel into the breech.
The shooter then placed a match
in a device that was attached to the
breech. This "matchlock" held the
match in an S-shaped lever known as
a serpentine. After lighting the match,
the shooter depressed the trigger,
lowering the match to a pan of finely
ground powder known as primer.
If all went as planned, the primer
ignited, causing an explosion that
propelled the ball in the direction of
the target.

In due course, designers came
up with a more advanced spring-
loaded matchlock that moved the

POWDER PLAY

Soldiers armed with matchlock muskets carried a supply of gunpowder in a large flask or a bandoleer of smaller containers. The larger style of flask was bell shaped and often constructed of iron and wood with a fabric covering. The soldier tipped out the proper amount of powder by means of a nozzle at the narrow end of the flask. In the bandoleer version, the musketeer filled small flasks with enough powder to fire his gun once and attached them to a beltlike strap that crossed his torso.

Hi Nawa Jyu

The Japanese only embraced gunpowder weapons after they saw how efficient muskets were on the battlefields in the late 1500s. Eventually they produced highly decorated matchlocks (called *hi nawa jyu*) that signified power and status.

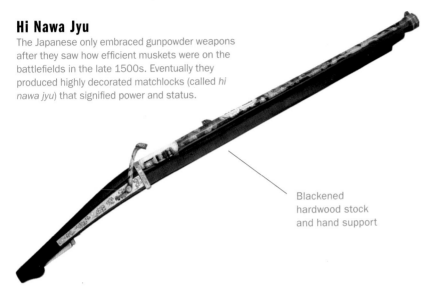

Blackened
hardwood stock
and hand support

serpentine more swiftly and reliably. But the matchlock mechanism didn't overcome the problems of keeping the match lit in poor weather or preventing the flame from touching the powder prematurely, a common cause of accidental discharge and shooter injury. Another hazard: The light of the smoldering match and ignited powder could give away a soldier's position to the enemy.

Despite its shortcomings, the matchlock remained popular through the early 1700s, in large part because it was relatively simple to operate and inexpensive to make. Some arquebuses were refitted with matchlocks, but as the technology improved, a sleeker triggered weapon, known as a musket (from the French *mosquette*) became increasingly common on European battlefields. King Henry VIII of England ordered 1,500 matchlock guns from craftsmen in the Venetian Republic in 1544. Many of these prized weapons were

lost, having seen little if any service in Henry's army, when the monarch's flagship, the *Mary Rose,* sank the following year in the Battle of Solent.

A Design Evolution

Matchlock designs varied. Some muskets in the 16th century had mechanisms similar to early crossbows, with longer levers that the user pulled upward instead of triggers that moved from front to rear. After Portuguese forces introduced matchlock muskets to Japan, local gunsmiths began producing a version with a short, curved stock and beautiful brass inlay, known as the *hi nawa jyu.* Combatants in the English Civil War (1642–1651) used more workmanlike muskets that were lighter and easier to handle. Later matchlock muskets, with their more attractive finishes and formfitting wooden stocks, began to resemble what we would recognize today as a long gun.

A LONG TRANSITION

Between the middle of the 15th century and the dawn of the 20th, warring nations increasingly integrated guns into their arsenals.

1300

1400

1440s Ottoman infantry troops adopted matchlock arms from Hungarians, setting the stage for the weapons to spread through the Turkish empire.

1500

1544 Henry VIII acquired 1,500 matchlock muskets from the Venetians. The British king then lost some of his new arsenal in a shipwreck in 1545.

1600

1550s In a transition from swords and bows, Japanese military leaders began arming soldiers with the *hi nawa jyu,* a weapon adapted from Portuguese muskets.

1700

1640s During the English Civil War, musketeers, vulnerable to charging cavalry, required protection by infantry.

1800

1900s Illustrating the staying power of older technology, nomad Tibetan forces continued to rely on matchlocks in conflicts with Chinese invaders.

1900

Matchlocks

BOTH THE IGNITION MECHANISM THAT HELD THE
SMOLDERING MATCHCORD AND THE GUN ITSELF
COULD BE REFERRED TO AS MATCHLOCKS.

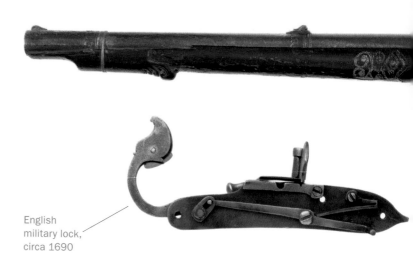

Once a shooter pulled the trigger of a matchlock, an S-shaped lever forced the matchcord into a pan of priming powder. When the powder was lit, it produced a flash to ignite the main charge. Even with the new ignition device, weapons still were muzzle loaded using a ramrod.

English military lock, circa 1690

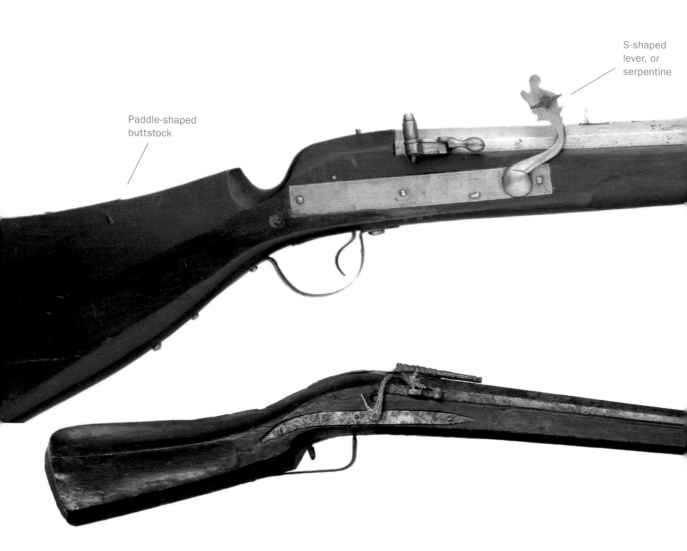

Paddle-shaped buttstock

S-shaped lever, or serpentine

◄ **MATCHLOCK MUSKET**

Country: Sri Lanka

Date: 1690

Barrel Length: 27 1/2in

Caliber: .90

The butt of this ornately carved handgun could rest against the shoulder or chest.

▼ **MATCHLOCK MUSKET**

Country: Austria or Germany

Date: late 17th century

Barrel Length: 47 1/2in

Caliber: .90

The tapering barrel was fit with rear and front sights.

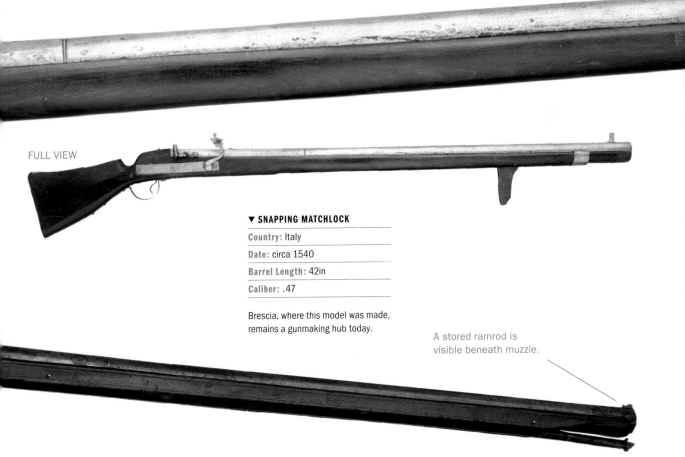

FULL VIEW

▼ **SNAPPING MATCHLOCK**

Country: Italy

Date: circa 1540

Barrel Length: 42in

Caliber: .47

Brescia, where this model was made, remains a gunmaking hub today.

A stored ramrod is visible beneath muzzle.

Sporting and Hunting Guns Proliferate

FOR ARISTOCRATS AND MERCHANTS, BEAUTIFUL
WEAPONS BECAME STATUS SYMBOLS.

By the mid 16th century, royal, aristocratic, and merchant-class weapon owners were commissioning long guns for nonmilitary sporting purposes. With increasingly elaborate features, these firearms nodded to their owners' success and social position. Animal-image inlays of bronze, gold, horn, or mother-of-pearl became popular. In Germany and Austria, craftsmen grew skilled not only at ornamentation, but also in advancing the mechanics of the matchlock and its successors, the wheellock and flintlock.

Through the 17th and 18th centuries, most sporting and hunting weapons, like most military guns, remained smoothbore, meaning the interior of the barrel was not "rifled" with spiral rifling grooves, and fired a solid lead ball. For hunting birds, rabbits, and other small game, sportsmen loaded their smoothbore guns with "shot," a small amount of lead pellets that upon firing would spread into a cloud of pellets called "a pattern" that could bring down fast-moving prey of modest size.

In time, gunsmiths incorporated a technique called rifling, first introduced in the 15th century, which involved boring grooves on the inside of gun barrels. Originally the procedure had been designed to reduce powder residue from building up in the barrel. But 17th and 18th century gunmakers discovered that rifling offered another advantage: Parallel spiral grooves caused the ball, or bullet, to spin in flight, vastly improving accuracy. A fraction of rich European sportsmen paid to have their muskets rifled to improve hunting efficiency, and small, specialized army units also carried limited numbers of rifles. Still, the procedure was difficult and expensive to execute and rifling remained rare until the fabrication advances of the Industrial Revolution.

A miquelet lock, an early form of the flintlock created by the Spanish

Gold stock inlaid with coral and silver

A SOCIAL MEDIUM

During the Middle Ages, the hunt for food evolved into a social activity, guns included, for the upper classes. Aristocrats adopted a stylized version of hunting as a sport, viewing it an honorable use of their leisure time and a manly form of competition. Women, too, were invited along to shoot, and did so in all their finery.

But the shift to hunting as recreation for the wealthy also created social friction. Where the landed aristocracy claimed exclusive rights to feudal territory, they found themselves at odds with commoners who continued to hunt for subsistence purposes. The legendary outlaw Robin Hood acquired his heroic status, in part, for hunting "the King's deer."

◄ **JEFFERSON'S MUSKET**

Country:	Tunisia
Date:	1789
Barrel Length:	84in
Caliber:	.69

The Bey of Tunisia gave this musket to President Thomas Jefferson in 1805.

Hunting and Sporting Guns

FROM THE 16TH TO 18TH CENTURIES,
LONG GUNS SPREAD ACROSS EUROPE.

Regional preferences were reflected in design features as well as style of firing mechanism. In Scotland, the snaphance was popular, while in Italian and German lands, gunmakers favored the wheellock. For large game, some hunters opted for rifles, which were more powerful than smoothbore shotguns and fired a single, large-caliber bullet.

Buttstock indented for fingers

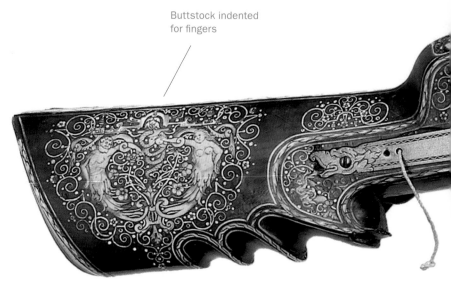

▼ SNAPHAUNCE GUN

Country: Scotland

Date: 1614

Barrel Length: 38in

Caliber: .45

The stock and shoulder butt are made of Brazilian wood.

Decorative silver inlay

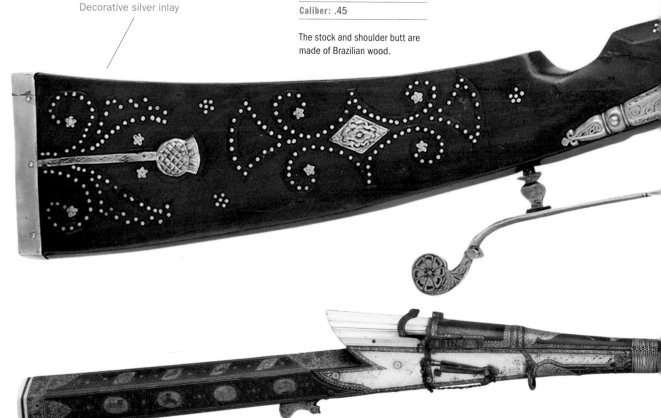

FULL VIEW

The barrel is ornamented with raised bands.

▲ MATCHLOCK GUN

Country: Germany

Date: 1621

Barrel Length: 48in

Caliber: .567

The narrow Flemish barrel has a large V-shaped backsight and flared muzzle.

FULL VIEW

▼ MATCHLOCK GUN

Country: India

Date: 17th century

Barrel Length: 41 3/4in

Caliber: .65

Nearly 10 pounds, this steel-barrel gun is embellished with silver, gold, copper, and ivory.

3 | AN ERA OF EXPERIMENTATION

NEW TECHNOLOGY LAID THE GROUNDWORK FOR MODERN PISTOLS AND
REVOLVERS AND INTRODUCED FEARS ABOUT GUNS AND CRIME.

During the Thirty Years' War among European powers, King Gustavus Adolphus of Sweden was killed in battle in 1632 by Catholic imperial forces using wheellock pistols.

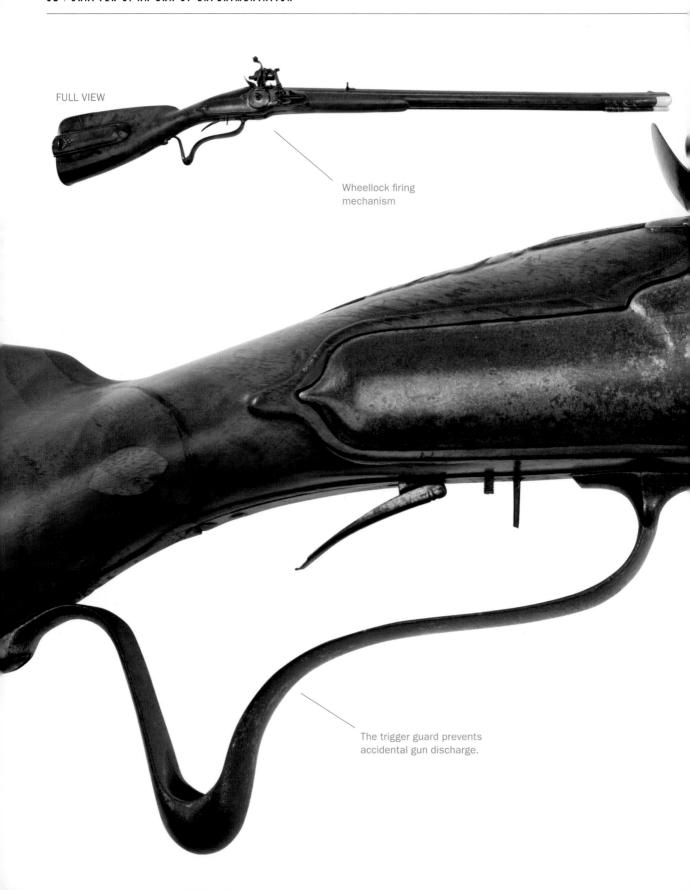

FULL VIEW

Wheellock firing
mechanism

The trigger guard prevents
accidental gun discharge.

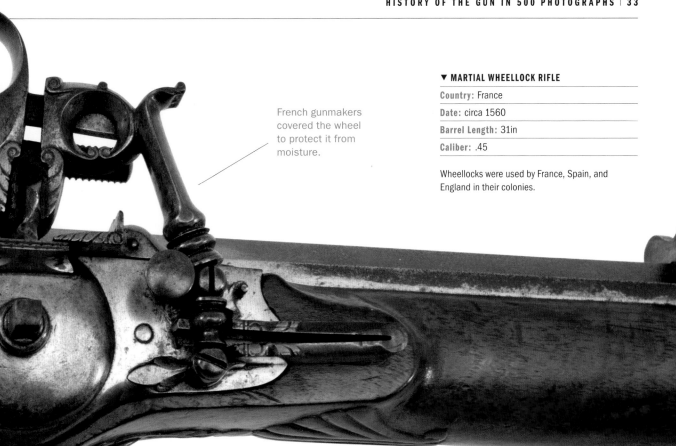

French gunmakers covered the wheel to protect it from moisture.

▼ MARTIAL WHEELLOCK RIFLE

Country:	France
Date:	circa 1560
Barrel Length:	31in
Caliber:	.45

Wheellocks were used by France, Spain, and England in their colonies.

The Arrival of the Wheellock and Flintlock

NEW IGNITION-AND-FIRING DEVICES MADE GUNS MORE
PORTABLE AND PAVED THE WAY FOR PISTOLS AND REVOLVERS.

The 16th century marked an inflection point in the development of firearms, thanks to a new generation of ignition-and-firing devices and the introduction of smaller, easier to carry weapons.

Until that time, the predominant lighting-and-shooting mechanism for muskets was the matchlock, which used a smoldering cord and priming powder. The guns were sturdy and simple to operate, but had limitations: The cord and powder were vulnerable to wind and rain; the burning cord alerted targets to the location of the gunman; and the complicated loading and firing process meant swift-moving cavalry couldn't rely on them. As the 1500s progressed, gunsmiths began experimenting with a new device, the wheellock, which ignited the powder internally without a match cord.

The change meant less effort was required to load and conceal guns and that they were available to fire at a moment's notice. The new technology also laid the groundwork for modern handguns—pistols and revolvers—and introduced new fears about the use of guns in crime and political assassination.

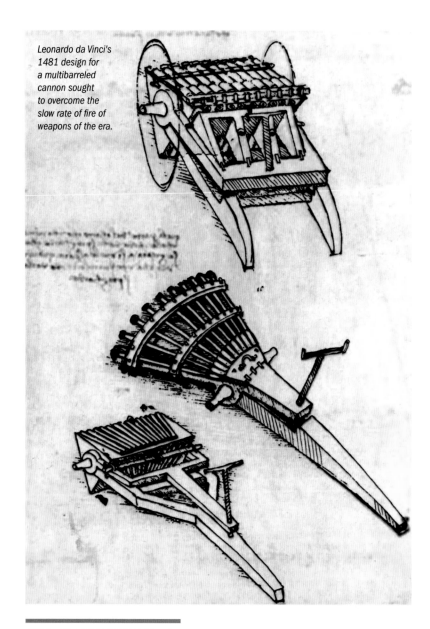

Leonardo da Vinci's 1481 design for a multibarreled cannon sought to overcome the slow rate of fire of weapons of the era.

ARMS AND THE RENAISSANCE MAN

Leonardo da Vinci (1452–1519) recorded many ideas for improving weaponry, though it would be centuries before engineering technology would catch with his vision. Field cannon of the era, for example, were difficult to reload, and there was a lag between blasts. Leonardo suggested a triple-barreled artillery piece where each barrel would be loaded separately, but all three fired simultaneously. In the 20th century, designers included multibarrel weapons in warships, military airplanes, and rocket launchers.

Similarly, Leonardo's idea for an armored car—one that could move in any direction and bristled with powerful weaponry—anticipated the modern tank. Leonardo imagined his machine would be powered by eight men inside the car who would turn cranks to rotate the wheels. He also considered using horses to make his armored car move but dropped the idea because the animals would be difficult to control within the vehicle.

The Da Vinci Codex

Some scholars attribute the essential idea for the wheellock to Leonardo da Vinci, the Renaissance polymath who kept detailed notebooks of his ideas and inventions. There are drawings of what looks like a wheellock device for a gun in Leonardo's Codex Atlanticus, a 12-volume work assembled in the 16th century that set out the inventor's ideas on astronomy, hydraulics, musical instruments, and more. Other historians trace the invention of the wheellock to an anonymous German craftsman whose mechanism appeared in a volume published in 1505. The German hypothesis suggests that the "Loffelholz Drawings," a collection of designs of uncertain provenance, may contain ideas that predate those of Leonardo.

Whoever deserves credit—and in

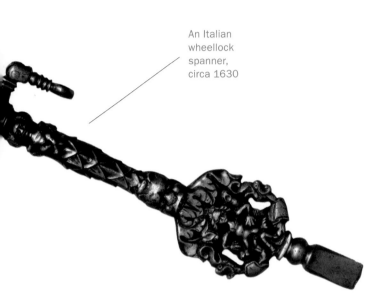

An Italian
wheellock
spanner,
circa 1630

all likelihood it should be shared—the earliest wheellocks seem to have been inspired by the clever notion of attaching a tinder lighter to the side of a musket to provide a means of igniting the gun's powder supply. (Imagine a rudimentary cigarette lighter or the utility lighter used to start a backyard grill.) The key components were a hammerlike piece known as the "dog" or "dog's head" that held a piece of iron pyrite and a spring-loaded steel wheel.

In preparation to fire, the shooter wound the wheel with a key, or "spanner," putting tension on the spring. When the trigger was pulled, the wheel released, struck the iron pyrite and generated a shower of sparks. The trigger pull simultaneously opened the pan holding the priming powder, which when lit sent a flash through a touchhole on the side of the gun

barrel. When the main powder charge in the breech ignited, gases were released that propelled the bullet.

The design evolution helped shift conflict on the battlefield. The new guns, albeit expensive to produce, were portable, which made it feasible to arm a cavalry unit. By the 1520s, designers were focusing on the wheellock and creating smaller guns—pistols—that could be operated easily with one hand.

Since each wheellock weapon could be fired only once before requiring an elaborate reloading procedure, well-equipped cavalry members began to carry two pistols. Some also added a smaller, more manageable version of the musket known as a "carbine." So armed, a horseman could get off three shots in quick succession, making him a far more lethal threat than ever before.

AN EVOLUTIONARY ERA

As handguns became smaller, they played a larger role on the battlefield.

1400

1450

1495 Leonardo da Vinci included what might be the earliest sketches of a wheellock ignition device in his Codex Atlanticus, a compilation of his ideas and sketches.

1500

1517 Fearing that the spread of wheellock pistols would lead to crime, Austrian emperor Maximilian I decreed what are thought to be among the earliest gun-control laws.

1550

1560S The Northern European snaphance gun lock debuted. It was simpler and more reliable than the traditional wheellock.

1600

1584 William, Prince of Orange, was assassinated with a flintlock pistol, underscoring how smaller, concealable weapons could enable crime.

1650

1632 Protestant King Gustavus Adolphus of Sweden was killed by Imperial Catholic forces using wheellock pistols during the Thirty Years' War among European powers.

1700

Wheellock Long Guns

WITH ORNATE DECORATIONS, THESE LONG GUNS
SAW ONLY LIMITED USE AS MILITARY WEAPONS.

The wheellock was an internal ignition system that protected the gunpowder from weather conditions. A steel wheel rotated against a sliver of iron pyrite to produce sparks which flashed through a touchhole to light the main gunpowder charge. Sixteenth and 17th century wheellock long guns, used primarily for hunting, had barrels that could exceed 40 inches, allowing the powder charge to burn completely and provide greater propulsion and accuracy. Most of these weapons were smoothbore muzzle-loaders.

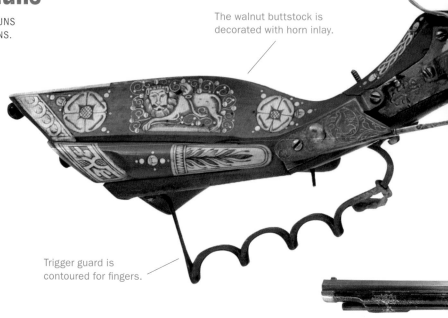

The walnut buttstock is decorated with horn inlay.

Trigger guard is contoured for fingers.

▲ **WHEELLOCK SPORTING GUN**

Country:	Germany
Date:	circa 1620
Barrel length::	46 1/2in
Caliber:	.50

Wheellock cover engraved with an angel

FULL VIEW

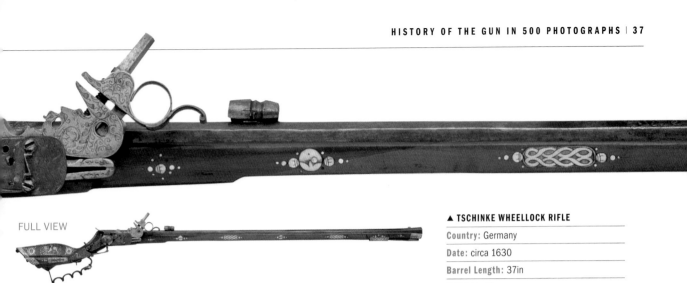

FULL VIEW

▲ TSCHINKE WHEELLOCK RIFLE

Country: Germany

Date: circa 1630

Barrel Length: 37in

Caliber: .33

The lock on this rifle is distinguished by its external wheel and mainspring.

▲ HUNTING RIFLE

Country: Germany

Date: mid 17th century

Barrel Length: 32 3/4in

The walnut stock is decorated with inlaid silver wire and appliqué.

The stock is inlaid with silver birds and flowers.

▼ **WHEELLOCK PISTOL**

Country: Italy

Date: circa 1635

Barrel Length: 10 1/5in

Caliber: .525

Giovanni Battista Francino, who belonged to a distinguished gunsmith family in Brescia, Italy, made this 1 pound, 11 ounce pistol.

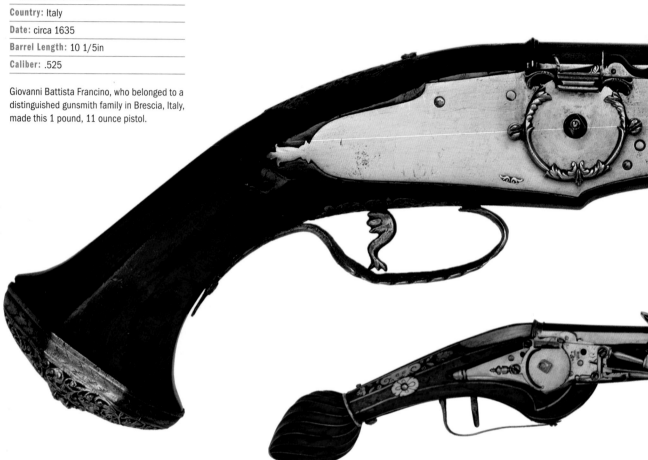

The Handgun Makes Its Debut

EARLY PISTOLS, WHICH WERE EASIER TO SHOOT WHILE ON THE MOVE, WERE POPULAR WITH BOTH CAVALRY UNITS AND OUTLAWS.

The pistol, a term likely derived from the Italian gunmaking center of Pistoia, combined wheellock technology with a short barrel and downward-angled grip that facilitated aiming while on the move. Though wheellock pistols and carbines were generally too expensive to be manufactured in sufficient numbers for ordinary infantry, they became the weapons of choice for elite members of the cavalry and prized possessions of the wealthy.

The new guns' ornamentation added to their allure. Some were inlaid with mother-of-pearl and steel-wire scrollwork, while others were designed with large round pommels at the base of the grip, a decorative flourish that made the weapon easier to pull out of a coat pocket or saddle holster, where they were carried by mounted troops and civilian owners.

The smaller, more concealable guns inadvertently empowered another category of armed men. Bandits, highwaymen, and political assassins

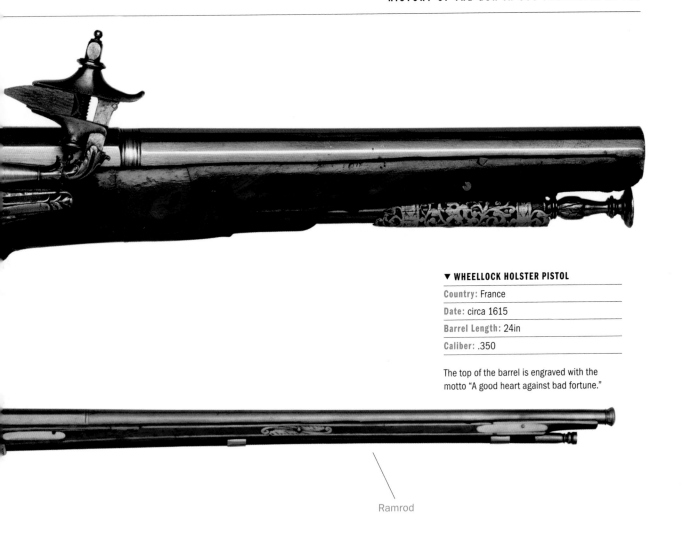

▼ **WHEELLOCK HOLSTER PISTOL**

Country: France

Date: circa 1615

Barrel Length: 24in

Caliber: .350

The top of the barrel is engraved with the motto "A good heart against bad fortune."

Ramrod

adopted the pistol, which was easily hidden beneath a cloak. In 1584, an assassin used a wheellock pistol to shoot Dutch leader William the Silent in one of the first political killings with a handgun.

Historians associate the emerging threat of gun crimes in the 16th century to the first

Smaller, more concealable guns inadvertently empowered bandits and highwaymen.

generation of what we today refer to as gun-control laws. Emperor Maximilian I, for example, declared restrictions on carrying wheellock weapons in Austria in 1517. In later years, similar laws spread throughout the Holy Roman Empire, and several Italian states adopted curbs by the 1530s.

Wheellock Handguns

THE FIRST TRUE HANDGUNS TAKE THEIR PLACE NEXT TO BULKIER MUSKETS.

Sixteenth century wheel-lock designs allowed guns to be carried primed and ready to fire, giving rise to a weapon that could be used with one hand. Cavalrymen had a weapon they could fire from horseback without dismounting. But outlaws saw the benefit of a concealable firearm, and European jurisdictions enacted bans on handguns as an anticrime measure—the forerunner of modern gun control.

Forged and hammer-welded lock

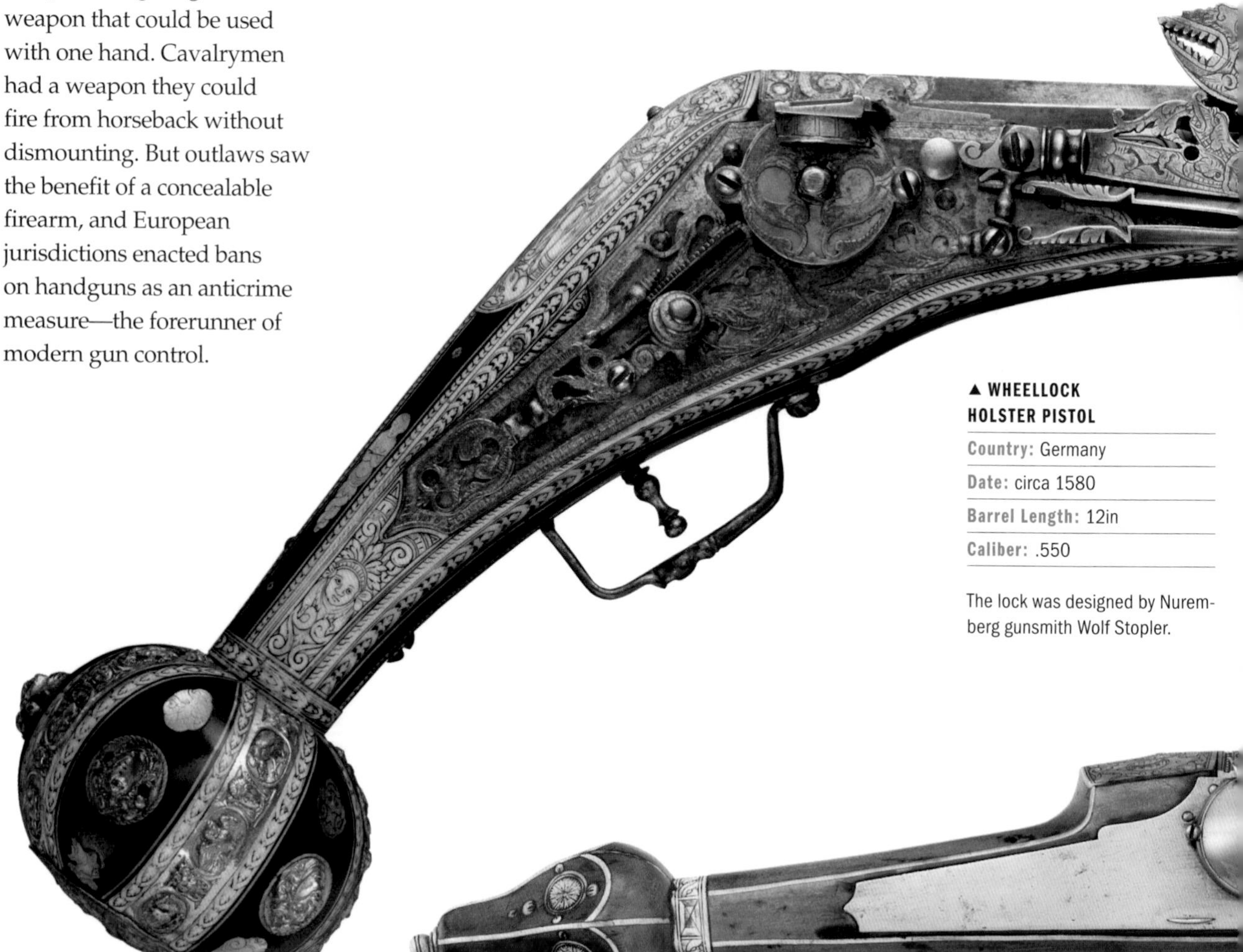

▲ **WHEELLOCK HOLSTER PISTOL**

Country: Germany

Date: circa 1580

Barrel Length: 12in

Caliber: .550

The lock was designed by Nuremberg gunsmith Wolf Stopler.

▲ WHEELLOCK PISTOL

Origin: probably Dutch

Date: circa 1550

Barrel Length: 23in

Caliber: .40

Gold Damascus-style decoration on the top of the barrel suggests the work of Damianus de Nerve or Diego de Caias.

Splayed barrels resemble a duck's foot.

▶ DUCK'S FOOT PISTOL

Country: Germany

Date: circa 1580

Main Barrel: 11in

Caliber: .600

A volley of bullets could hit multiple opponents with the pull of a single trigger.

One of a matched pair of pistols made for the bodyguard of the Prince-Elector of Saxony

▲ HOLSTER PISTOL

Country: Germany

Date: 1610

Barrel length: 18in

Caliber: .580

Wheellock Combination Weapons

MAKERS CREATED DUAL-PURPOSE WEAPONS WITH MACE, AXE, MILITARY FORK, HALBERD AND OTHER FEATURES.

As the 16th century progressed, gunmakers began combining wheellock-pistol technology with conventional weaponry. In case the pistol misfired, the soldier could resort to one of the weapon's other functions—for example, pulling a rider off his steed with a handle. Though the multipurpose weapons were often clumsy and difficult to use, they were prized as curiosities.

The halberd was used from the 14th to the 16th century.

Pistol barrels mounted on both sides of spear shaft

▲ MACE AND WHEELLOCK PISTOL

Country: Germany

Date: circa 1560

Length: 22 7/10in

Weight: 3 1/4lb

The pistol barrel forms the shaft of the mace; the six-point flange features cloverleaf cutouts.

The curved claw originally was attached to a hammerhead.

▶ COMBINED HALBERD AND DOUBLE-BARRELLED PISTOL

Country: Germany

Date: circa 1590

Barrel Length: 27 1/4in

Bore: .35

A combined spear, axe, and gun make this weapon a triple threat. The hook on the right could grasp a mounted enemy.

◀ MILITARY FORK AND WHEEL-LOCK PISTOL

Country: Germany

Date: circa 1590

Caliber: .35

The upper portion of the long, narrow handle, also called a haft, is inlaid with masks and flowers made from stag antlers.

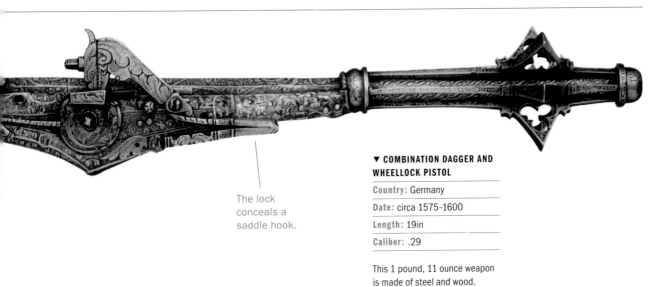

The lock conceals a saddle hook.

▼ COMBINATION DAGGER AND WHEELLOCK PISTOL

Country: Germany

Date: circa 1575–1600

Length: 19in

Caliber: .29

This 1 pound, 11 ounce weapon is made of steel and wood.

► COMBINED AXE AND WHEELLOCK PISTOL

Origin: Germany or Iberia

Date: early 17th century

Overall Length: 21 4/5in

Bore: .31

There are five barrels embedded in the axe head; they are concealed by a hinged cover.

Barrel openings

Hinged cover

FULL VIEW

The Flintlock Revolution

EUROPEAN DESIGNERS USED A STEEL STRIKING STONE TO
CREATE SPARKS AND STREAMLINE GUNMAKING.

By the late 16th century, gunsmiths in northern Europe were devising improved methods of generating sparks to ignite priming powder. The main advance involved using hardened steel against natural flint.

The first of these was the "snaphance," or "snaphaunce" (from the Dutch word for "pecking bird"), which appeared in the 1560s. In this simpler and more reliable variation of a gun lock, the jaws of a spring-loaded "cock" holding a fragment of flint moved forward at the pull of the trigger and struck a piece of steel, creating sparks that lit powder in the priming pan. If a shot was successful, the fire ignited the main powder load in the breech and the bullet was released. If the process failed and the bullet didn't launch, it was labeled "a flash in the pan," a phrase that later came to suggest noise or pyrotechnics with little or no lasting effect.

Seizing on the promise of flint, gunsmiths in France and elsewhere in Europe began to develop what would become known as the flintlock. In this streamlined design, the pan cover and steel-striking piece were

The L-shaped steel frizzen is part of the flintlock firing mechanism.

▼ **MODEL 1787 FLINTLOCK MUZZLE-LOADING CARBINE**

Country: Germany

Date: circa 1790

Barrel Length: 27in

British Duck Foot Pistol

Flintlock devices were used well into the 18th century in combination with a variety of eccentric pistol designs, none more memorable than the "duck foot." With four barrels, the weapon could fire a quartet of bullets simultaneously, if not necessarily accurately. Prison wardens and ship captains brandished the weapons to deter unruly prisoners or sailors. Only a limited number of duck foot pistols were ever made, and those that remain have become prized collectors' items.

combined into a single component and the overall number of gun parts were reduced to fewer than 20—half as many as the wheellock. In time, gunsmiths also moved the mechanical striking parts to the interior of the lock, where they were less exposed to the elements.

The flintlock coexisted for centuries with the more entrenched matchlock and wheellock guns. Early iterations can be seen in paintings of the 1620s by the Flemish Baroque artist Peter Paul Rubens, and flintlocks saw action during the English Civil War (1642–1651). They continued to catch on with military men and others, and by the 18th century, flintlock technology was widely embraced.

The fact that the flintlock

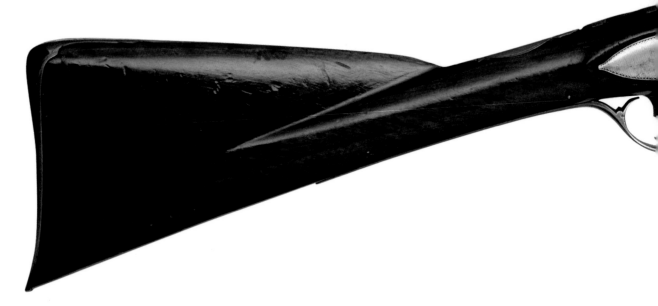

devices could be attached to most any type of weapon and that they were moderately priced made them popular with Europeans and in European colonial territories. They also attracted interest from nonaristocrats: Hunters began to equip long guns with flintlock firing mechanisms, and duelists clashing over perceived slights used matched pairs of decorated flintlock pistols to settle scores.

While most flintlocks continued to be muzzle loaded, by the 1700s some gunsmiths made pistols loaded via the breech. The user unscrewed the barrel and inserted powder and ball at the breech, a process that sounds arduous but actually proved more efficient than the traditional use of a ramrod via the muzzle. A skilled gunman could fire several rounds in a minute with a breech-loading firearm.

Distinctive Styles and Models

During this era, the trade of gunsmith flourished, and craftsmen adorned weapons with ornamental carvings, silver mountings, engravings, and decorative inlays. By the late 18th century, sophisticated gun-smiths in Britain, the American colonies, and France had developed distinctive styles and models.

John Waters of Birmingham, for example, produced a famous blunderbuss pistol (from the Dutch *donderbus,* or "thunder gun") that fired batches of shot, or small lead balls, from a flared muzzle. The wide mouth of the barrel allowed the shot to spread in flight, increasing the chances of hitting one or more targets. Below the brass barrel, Waters attached a spring-loaded blade that snapped out upon the pull of a secondary trigger. The miniature bayonet allowed the pistol user to close in for the kill if his initial shot didn't finish the job.

Craftsmen with London's Griffin & Tow made a pistol popular during the reign of Queen Anne (1665–1714) that had a tapered barrel and two triggers, one for each of the gun's locks. A small version of the weapon was known as a "muff pistol," suggesting that it could be concealed in the hand warmer of a lady fearing attack, or perhaps planning to commit one herself. Queen Anne–style pistols remained popular in the United Kingdom for the rest of the 18th century.

In the American colonies, a Scottish immigrant named James Hunter produced the first colonial-manufactured military pistol at the Rappahannock Forge in Virginia. Hunter's design imitated one used by the British Light Dragoons. The .69-caliber pistol had a nine-inch barrel and an elegant brass-capped pommel. Soldiers and sailors continued to use flintlock pistols, carbines, and muskets through the 1830s.

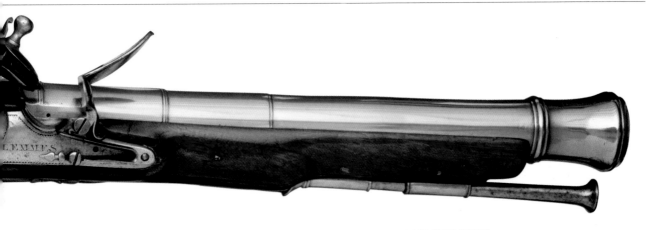

▲ FLINTLOCK BLUNDERBUSS

Country: Great Britain

Date: 1755–1760

Barrel Length: 12 1/2in

This muzzle-loading flintlock weighed 5 pounds, 13 ounces. The flared barrel opening was 1 1/6 inches.

THE FLINTLOCK ASSASSIN

William I, Prince of Orange (1533–1584), was also known as William the Silent. He overcame his famous reticence to serve as leader of the Dutch revolt against the Spanish Hapsburgs. That rebellion in turn led to the formation of the Dutch Republic in 1648.

William met an untimely end at the hand of a Burgundian named Balthasar Gerard, who regarded the prince as a traitor to King Philip II of Spain and to the Catholic Church. To execute his plot, Gerard engaged in an elaborate multiyear deception. After ingratiating himself with William, Gerard acquired a pair of flintlock pistols and shot his quarry dead in Delft in July 1584. Caught and imprisoned, Gerard met an even worse fate: live quartering and disembowelment, the removal of his heart, and separation of his head from his neck.

Early Flintlock Guns

MOVING ON FROM THE WHEELLOCK.

With early flintlocks, gunmakers streamlined traditional design, combining the pan cover and steel-striking piece into a single component and reducing the overall number of gun parts to fewer than 20—half as many as the wheellock. The term flintlock refers both to the ignition mechanism itself and to any firearm that incorporates the mechanism into its design.

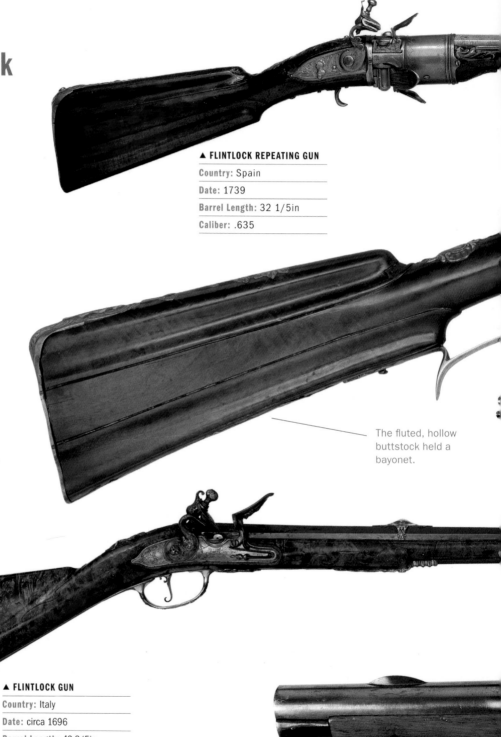

▲ **FLINTLOCK REPEATING GUN**

Country: Spain

Date: 1739

Barrel Length: 32 1/5in

Caliber: .635

The fluted, hollow buttstock held a bayonet.

▲ **FLINTLOCK GUN**

Country: Italy

Date: circa 1696

Barrel Length: 42 3/5in

Caliber: .675

This 7 pound, 6 ounce flintlock was made in Florence by Michele Lorenzoni.

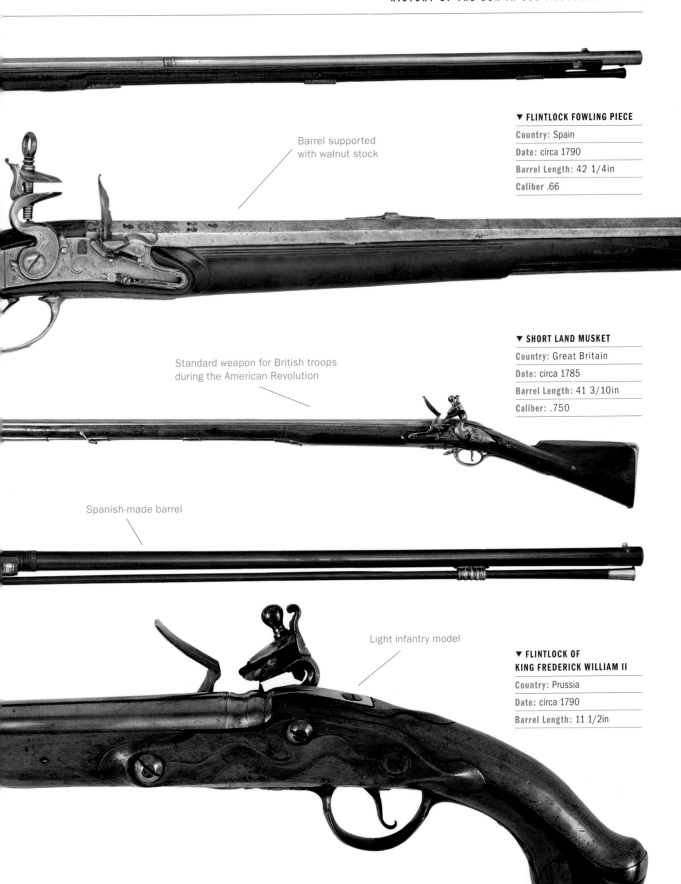

Barrel supported
with walnut stock

▼ FLINTLOCK FOWLING PIECE

Country: Spain

Date: circa 1790

Barrel Length: 42 1/4in

Caliber .66

Standard weapon for British troops
during the American Revolution

▼ SHORT LAND MUSKET

Country: Great Britain

Date: circa 1785

Barrel Length: 41 3/10in

Caliber: .750

Spanish-made barrel

Light infantry model

▼ FLINTLOCK OF
KING FREDERICK WILLIAM II

Country: Prussia

Date: circa 1790

Barrel Length: 11 1/2in

Later Flintlock Guns

THE FLINTLOCK REMAINED IN USE FOR MORE THAN TWO CENTURIES.

In the 17th and 18th centuries, the flintlock began replacing earlier firearm-ignition technology. Gunmakers produced the blunderbuss, flintlock long gun, and the smoothbore musket. The guns fired lead shot and were favored as defensive weapons by coachmen, innkeepers, and merchants.

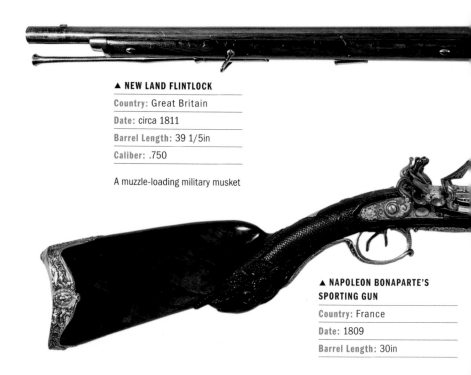

▲ NEW LAND FLINTLOCK

Country: Great Britain

Date: circa 1811

Barrel Length: 39 1/5in

Caliber: .750

A muzzle-loading military musket

▲ NAPOLEON BONAPARTE'S SPORTING GUN

Country: France

Date: 1809

Barrel Length: 30in

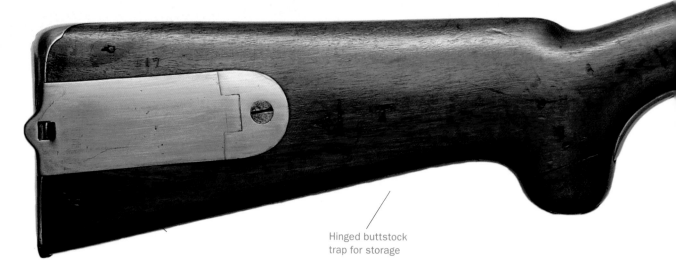

Hinged buttstock trap for storage

► FLINTLOCK MILITARY CARBINE

Country: France

Date: 1815

Barrel Length: 32 1/4in

Caliber: .71

This flintlock was likely used in Napolean's Hundred Days campaign.

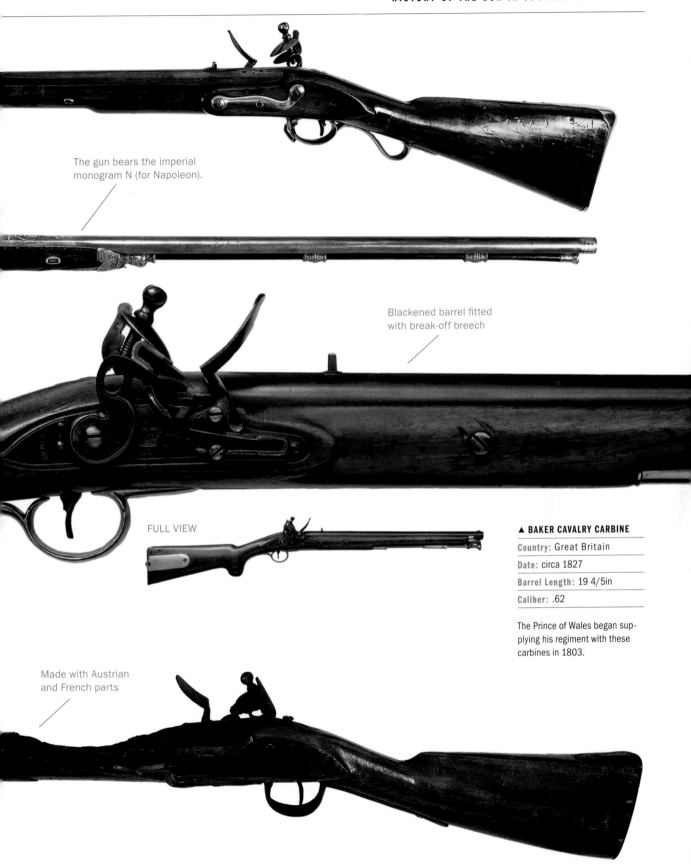

The gun bears the imperial monogram N (for Napoleon).

Blackened barrel fitted with break-off breech

FULL VIEW

Made with Austrian and French parts

▲ BAKER CAVALRY CARBINE

Country: Great Britain

Date: circa 1827

Barrel Length: 19 4/5in

Caliber: .62

The Prince of Wales began supplying his regiment with these carbines in 1803.

Dueling Pistols

FAMOUS MAKERS PRODUCED
FIREARMS IN CASED PAIRS.

As antagonists moved from swords to pistols to settle scores in the 18th century, gunmakers began designing more accurate dueling pistols, often in cased pairs. Some of the era's best known weapon designers, such as Londoners Robert Wogdon and brothers John and Joseph Manton, produced dueling pistols.

▼ PERCUSSION PISTOLS

Country:	Great Britain
Date:	1775–1885
Length:	14 1/2in

These silver-mounted pistols came with a leather powder flask and turnscrew.

Mahogany case
with brass handle

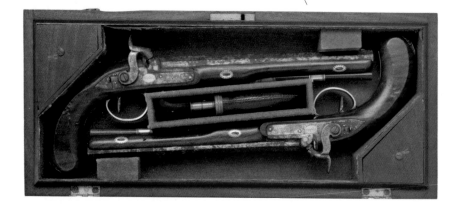

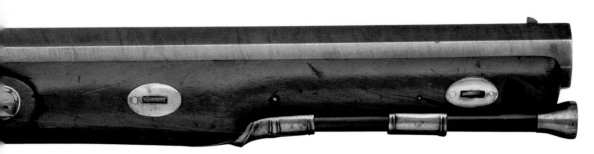

▲ SAW-HANDLE PISTOL

Country: Great Britain

Date: 1810–1815

Barrel Length: 9in

Mahogany case
lined with velvet

▼ FLINTLOCK PISTOLS

Country: Great Britain

Date: circa 1815

Length: 14 7/8in

The locks are engraved with border
ornament and sprays of foliage.

Blunderbusses and Carbines

THESE WEAPONS WERE EARLY VERSIONS OF THE SHOTGUN.

The blunderbuss flintlock was muzzle loaded with a large caliber to contain many balls or slugs. The gun was intended to be fired at short range. The flintlock carbine was usually smaller and lighter than a military musket. Some were intended for use by cavalry.

▲ **FLINTLOCK MILITARY BLUNDERBUSS**

Country: Great Britain

Date: circa 1781

The blunderbuss got its name from the Dutch term *donderbus*, meaning "thunder box" or "thunder gun."

Breech open for loading

▶ **FLINTLOCK BREECH-LOADING CARBINE**

Country: Great Britain

Date: circa 1810

Barrel Length: 20 1/5in

Bore: .66

Breech-loading guns reduced reloading time by eliminating the need to push powder and projectiles down the barrel.

▲ **FLINTLOCK BLUNDERBUSS**

Country: Great Britain

Date: circa 1790

Barrel Length: 13 7/10in

This brass-barrel blunderbuss features a top-mounted bayonet.

Three-sided bayonet

▼ **FLINTLOCK MUZZLE-LOADER**

Origin: Netherlands

Date: 1810

Bore: .51

Renowned gunmaker Guillaume Berleur most likely made this weapon for Napoleon's army.

First Empire–style stock with gilded thumb piece

European Flintlock Hunting Long Guns

GERMAN, BRITISH, AND ITALIAN CRAFTSMEN
WERE KNOWN FOR THEIR ENGRAVING WORK.

By the start of the 18th century, designers were not only producing visually arresting guns, they had developed flintlocks which could hit moving targets, including birds in flight, because the firing mechanism was faster.

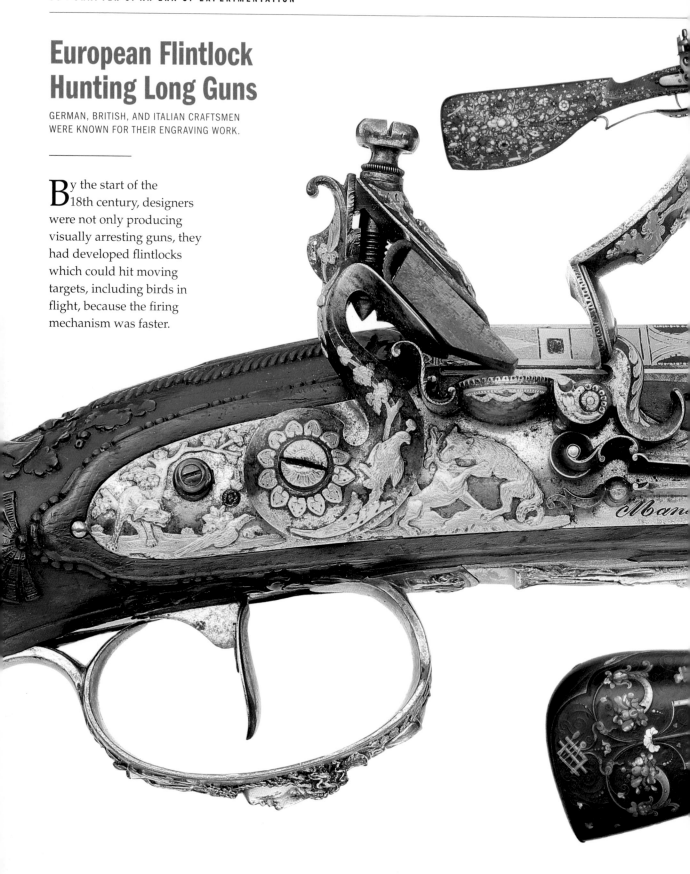

▲ **FLINTLOCK SPORTING GUN**

Country: Germany

Date: 1646

Barrel Length: 44in

Bore: .39

The full stock of this hunting gun is lavishly inlaid with yellow-stained staghorn designs.

▼ **FLINTLOCK SPORTING GUN**

Country: France

Date: circa 1802

Barrel Length: 38 1/4in

Caliber: .638

Decorated with hunting scenes and the king's portrait, this silver-mounted flintlock was a gift to Spain's King Charles IV from the French government.

FULL VIEW

▲ **FLINTLOCK SPORTING GUN**

Country: France

Date: circa 1675

Barrel Length: 46 1/2in

Caliber: .625

The Marquis de Croissy is said to have presented this exquisite firearm to the 7th Earl of Pembroke as a wedding gift in 1675.

Asia Flintlock Guns

JAPAN, INDIA AND THE OTTOMAN EMPIRE
PRODUCED EXTRAORDINARILY BEAUTIFUL GUNS.

Though firearms first appeared
in Japan in the 1200s, it took the
introduction of European models in
the 1600s to popularize them. The first
use of firearms in the Ottoman Empire
dates to at least the early 15th century.
Gunmaking flourished across Asia in
the 1700s and 1800s.

▼ **FLINTLOCK GUN**

Country:	India
Date:	circa 1780
Barrel Length:	39 3/4in
Caliber:	.690

A ribbon pattern runs the length
of the browned barrel, which is
octagonal at the breech.

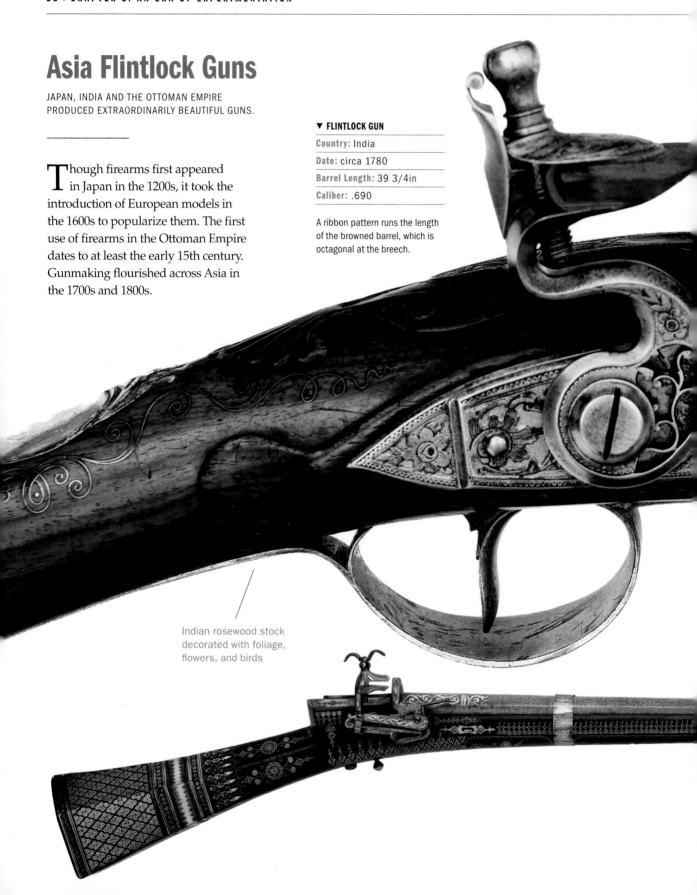

Indian rosewood stock
decorated with foliage,
flowers, and birds

Iranian-made full stock with enameled gold mounts

▲ FLINTLOCK RIFLE

Origin: India

Date: circa 1835

Barrel Length: 42 3/4in

Caliber: .55

The Damascus-steel barrel has a gilt muzzle in the shape of a dragon's head with eyes set with rubies and emeralds.

FULL VIEW

◀ FLINTLOCK RIFLE

Country: Turkey

Date: 19th century

Turkish rifles of this period were profusely inlaid with gold, silver, and bands of colored ivory.

4 | COMING TO AMERICA

WHEN THE REVOLUTIONARY WAR ERUPTED, SKILLED MARKSMEN ARMED WITH
LONG RIFLES WERE ABLE TO HIT BRITISH TARGETS FROM 300 YARDS.

After British forces bayoneted American leader Hugh Mercer during the Battle of Princeton, General George Washington arrived to rally the troops. Painting by William Tylee Ranney, 1848.

MARKSMAN STYLE

The colonial militia-men who became soldiers in the Continental Army arrived for battle against the British in a variety of sartorial styles. For his forces, General George Washington favored the traditional hunting shirt popular in his home state of Virginia. A homespun garment, the hunting shirt was made from basic linen, fit loosely and allowed easy movement. In cold weather, better-equipped American soldiers also donned a wool overcoat. Washington noted an additional benefit: The hunting shirt, he observed, communicated "no small terror to the enemy, who think every such person is a complete marksman."

The New World

COLONIAL GUNSMITHS ADOPTED RIFLING, A TECHNIQUE FROM 15TH-CENTURY GERMANY THAT IMPROVED A GUN'S ACCURACY.

Images of the pilgrims of the 17th century often show settlers with flintlock blunderbusses, but in all likelihood the early colonists brought with them more basic matchlocks, with perhaps the rare wheellock thrown in for variety. By the early 18th century, however, American gunsmiths, many of German descent, were producing flintlock weapons the colonists could call their own. Settlers used firearms for military service and personal protection, and also for hunting, an important source of food and commercially valuable pelts in the heavily forested "new world." Marksmanship became an

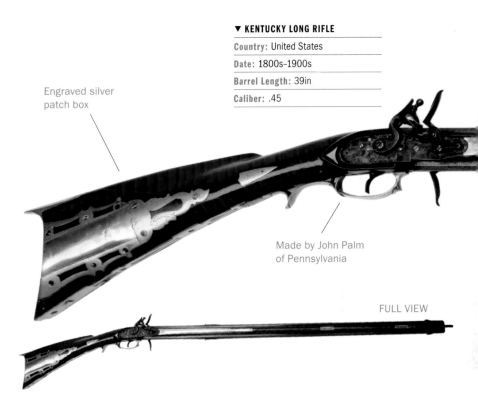

Engraved silver patch box

▼ KENTUCKY LONG RIFLE

Country: United States	
Date: 1800s–1900s	
Barrel Length: 39in	
Caliber: .45	

Made by John Palm of Pennsylvania

FULL VIEW

important and honored skill.

One of the most notable American designs was the "long rifle," also known as the Ohio, Pennsylvania, or Kentucky rifle, depending on where the rifleman resided. Derivative of the classic German Jäger rifle ("hunter rifle"), the American versions evolved to have longer barrels for greater accuracy and slender wooden stocks that extended the full length of the barrel. The rear of the stock, held against the shooter's shoulder, had a gradual downward curve. Well-to-do colonists paid to have their long rifles decorated with pewter or brass inlays depicting animals or shapes such as hearts or stars.

As the designation "rifle" indicates, American gunsmiths sought enhanced accuracy by making the transition from smoothbore weapons to "rifled" long guns. In a smoothbore weapon, the ball fit loosely in the barrel. Once propelled by exploding gases, the round careered down the barrel, banging from side to side and emerging at an unpredictable angle from the muzzle. This effect made early pistols and muskets notoriously inaccurate.

Carving spiral grooves into the interior of the barrel, or rifling, caused the ball to spin gyroscopically, which kept it on a straight course over a far longer distance. German gunsmiths invented the technique back in the late 15th century, but because of the expense of precision metalworking and the talent required to do it well, rifles remained relatively rare. There were other downsides as well: Rifles were more susceptible to clogging because of powder residue, and tighter-fitting rifle balls were more difficult to load into weapons that for the most part were still muzzle-loaders.

Panic Among the Redcoats

When the Revolutionary War erupted in 1776, American forces included snipers and light infantry equipped

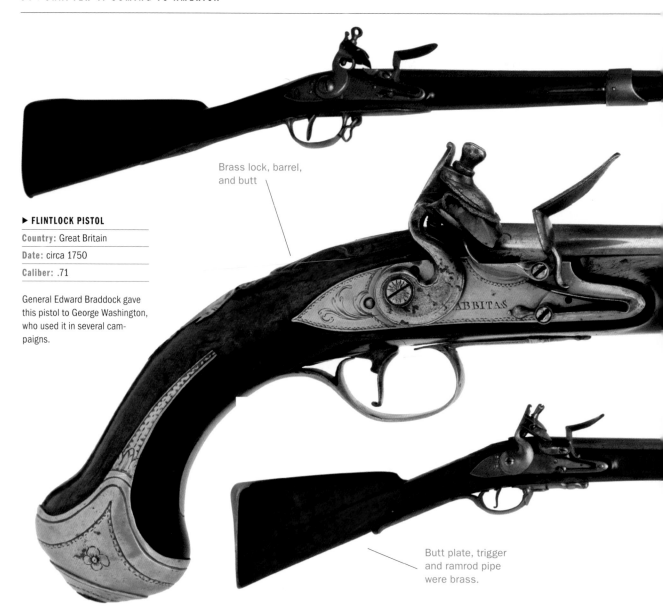

Brass lock, barrel, and butt

► **FLINTLOCK PISTOL**

Country: Great Britain

Date: circa 1750

Caliber: .71

General Edward Braddock gave this pistol to George Washington, who used it in several campaigns.

Butt plate, trigger and ramrod pipe were brass.

with long rifles. Skilled marksmen in specialized units could hit British targets at a range of 300 yards, compared to less than a third of that distance with a smoothbore musket. The ability of riflemen to target and kill British officers helped the Revolutionary forces disrupt their foes' command structure and spread panic among the redcoats.

But American soldiers with rifles still needed protection from larger infantry units armed with smoothbore muskets that were easier to operate. The Brown Bess, a British musket imported to the colonies, and later copied in the breakaway states, became a common weapon on the Revolutionary side. It could be loaded with a single ball or a cluster of shot. The Short Land Pattern version of the Brown Bess was, as the name implied, a shorter, lighter variation of the more common Long Land Pattern.

Bayonets remained vital firearm accoutrements throughout the Revolutionary War, as the musket's inaccuracy meant that many battles were decided by means of massive charges and hand-to-hand struggles to the death. Because of the absence of effective medicine, a tearing flesh wound rendered by bayonet was actually just as likely to be lethal as a puncture wound by small lead ball.

General George Washington,

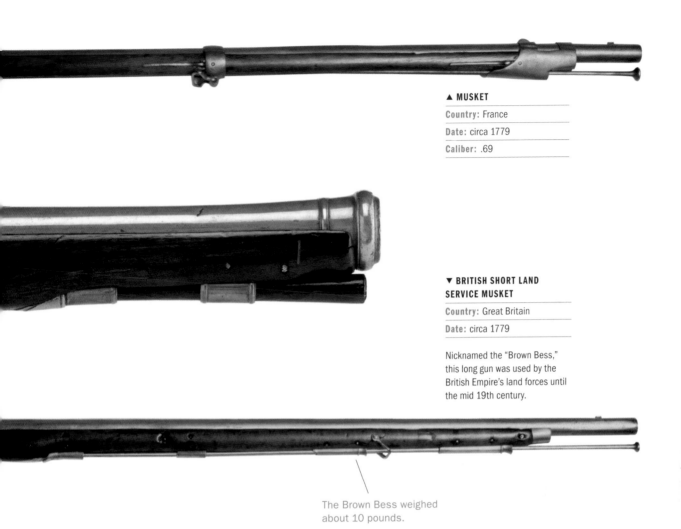

▲ MUSKET

Country: France

Date: circa 1779

Caliber: .69

▼ BRITISH SHORT LAND
SERVICE MUSKET

Country: Great Britain

Date: circa 1779

Nicknamed the "Brown Bess,"
this long gun was used by the
British Empire's land forces until
the mid 19th century.

The Brown Bess weighed
about 10 pounds.

interestingly, focused on the rifle's drawbacks: the expense of manufacture, slow reloading process, and need to do extensive training for those recruits not already skilled in hunting. While Washington urged limited use of rifle companies, other Revolutionary leaders showed more enthusiasm and scraped together the resources to outfit sharpshooting units that played significant roles in the battles of Saratoga and New Orleans.

CLUBBING THE ENEMY

During the 1600s and for centuries thereafter, troops generally fired their muskets in massive volleys similar to the waves of arrows launched by archers. Given the difficulty of aiming at a far-off target, musket men typically did not pause to reload, but instead followed a volley by charging at the enemy with bayonets. Infantry units generally did more lethal damage in hand-to-hand combat, stabbing and clubbing the enemy, than they did by firing their guns.

SPRINGFIELD: ARMORY FOR A NEW NATION

Beginning in the 17th century, colonial militia conducted training exercises on a bluff near the Connecticut River in Massachusetts. After the American Revolution began, military officer Henry Knox and George Washington established an armory on the site, in 1777, and it was used to supply forces in upstate New York.

1787 During a short-lived antitax and antidebt rebellion, former Revolutionary soldier Daniel Shays and his renegade forces tried to capture the armory but were repelled by Massachusetts government forces.

1812 The Springfield Armory produced muskets used by U.S. troops in the War of 1812 against Great Britain, a conflict sometimes referred to as a "second war of independence."

1845 After visiting the amory during his honeymoon, Henry Wadsworth Longfellow published "The Arsenal at Springfield," a poem that referenced racks of muskets as an antiwar metaphor.

1750 | 1800 | 1850

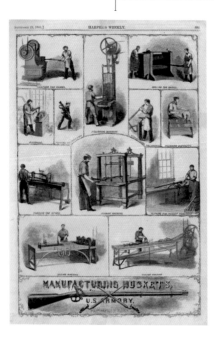

1795 Manufacture of firearms at the Springfield Armory began; it continued through the late 1960s.

1861–1865 The Springfield Model 1861, a Minié-type rifled musket, was used by Union forces and the Confederate States of America during the Civil War. It weighed about 9 pounds and was favored for its accuracy, reliability, and range.

1866–1871 Following the Civil War, the armory received permission to create an on-site collection of weapons that could be used by staff engineers for reference during the research and development process. In 1871, the collection opened to the public as a museum.

1962 The armory was designated a National Historic Landmark in 1962, then in 1964, U.S. secretary of defense Robert McNamara announced the armory would be closing. It shuttered its doors in 1968, with the National Park Service taking stewardship of the site and museum collection in 1978.

1900 The armory began a three-year process of replacing the Krag-Jorgensen magazine rifle. Work on the design continued until 1903, when the Model 1903 was officially approved. It was a standard military rifle for over three decades, and a special-use rifle through the Vietnam War.

1919 John Garand was hired to head the Model Shop and work on semi-automatic rifles and other small projects. The final design for the M1 was adopted in the mid 1930s and the gun was embraced by the U.S. military. By the end of World War II, the armory had produced 3.5 million semiautomatic Garands.

An Armory's Legacy

AMAZING INNOVATION STARTED WITH A COPY OF A FRENCH FLINTLOCK MUSKET.

Originally an arsenal for the Continental Army, the Springfield Armory became a full-fledged factory in 1795 on the order of President George Washington. His directive: produce flintlock muskets for his young nation. A year later, the armory issued a copy of a French Charville flintlock musket and over the next two centuries continued with innovations that spanned gunmaking and industrial production. Probably the most famous rifle ever produced by the armory was the M1 Garand.

Springfield's first weapon was a French-style flintlock.

Became standard issue for U.S. infantrymen in World War I

▲ MODEL 1903 RIFLE

Country: United States

Date: 1903–1974

Barrel Length: 24in

Caliber: .30

Over one million were made through World War I and into the 1930s.

▼ M1 GARAND

Country: United States

Date: 1937–1950s

Barrel Length: 24in

Caliber: .30

Over 13,500 employees worked 24 hours a day during World War II to produce this semiautomatic.

▲ **MODEL 1795**

Country: United States

Date: 1795–1845

Barrel Length: 44 1/2in

Caliber: .69

Used the Minié ball for ammunition

◄ **MODEL 1861 RIFLE MUSKET**

Country: United States

Date: 1862

Barrel Length: 40in

Caliber: .58

Featured a percussion ignition system and a rifled bore.

Developed to surpass the first bolt-action rifle used by the U.S. Army

A descendant of the M1 Garand

▲ **M14**

Country: United States

Date: 1957

Barrel Length: 22in

Caliber: .30

The rate of fire was superior to the slower Mauser used by German forces.

5 | THE ROAD TO THE REVOLVER

A NEW PERCUSSION-CAP FIRING MECHANISM HELPED PAVE THE WAY FOR DESIGNER
SAMUEL COLT AND HIS FAMOUS "GUN THAT WON THE WEST."

Colt workers in the Hartford, Connecticut, factory circa 1900. Employee numbers swelled from 2,400 to 15,000 between World War I and World War II.

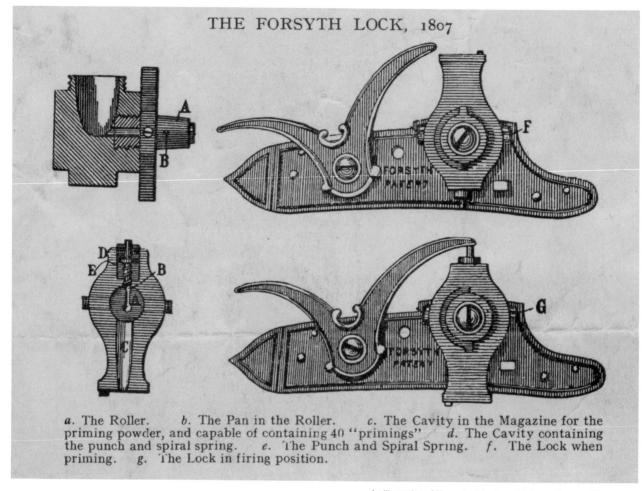

THE FORSYTH LOCK, 1807

a. The Roller.   *b.* The Pan in the Roller.   *c.* The Cavity in the Magazine for the priming powder, and capable of containing 40 "primings"   *d.* The Cavity containing the punch and spiral spring.   *e.* The Punch and Spiral Spring.   *f.* The Lock when priming.   *g.* The Lock in firing position.

An illustration of Alexander John Forsyth's innovative gun-firing system.

Weapons Evolution

PERCUSSION-CAP GUNS AND REPEAT-FIRE WEAPONS LAID
THE GROUNDWORK FOR THE NEXT BIG THING: THE REVOLVER.

By 1800, the flintlock had been in use for almost a century around the world. Under most circumstances, the device worked adequately, with flint hitting steel to produce sparks that ignited the priming powder. But when it was wet outside, dampened primer didn't always light, and even in ideal weather the delay between the lighting of powder in the pan and the ignition of the main charge made it difficult to hit a moving target.

In the first years of the 19th century, gunmakers began seeing if it was possible to ignite the main charge in other ways. One promising advance came from Scotland: In 1808, Scottish Presbyterian minister Alexander John Forsyth invented a delicate hammer-fired device, patented as the Forsyth Patent Percussion Sporting Gun, to be used in long guns for hunting birds.

Forsyth's weapon lead to the sturdier "percussion cap" guns that fired more rapidly and reliably in any weather. Their design relied on a small brass or copper cylinder with one closed end that held a tiny amount of explosive chemical and fit over a hollow metal "nipple" at the back of the gun barrel. Depressing the trigger released a hammer that struck the percussion cap, igniting the chemical primer and sending a flame to light the main powder charge. In 1814, Joshua Shaw, a British-born resident of Philadelphia, invented another version of the metallic percussion cap, one that relied on a mixture of fulminate of mercury, chlorate of potash, and ground glass.

Retrofitting Firearms

Early 19th-century gunsmiths fitted all types of firearms—pistols, muskets, carbines, and rifles—with percussion caps. Some owners of flintlock weapons had their guns overhauled to accommodate the new technology. The British military updated its Brown Bess muskets in this fashion in the 1830s and 1840s, while the U.S. Army introduced a percussion-cap carbine rifle. Despite its effectiveness in inclement weather, however, the new device's small size made it to difficult to operate during the chaos of actual combat or while riding on horseback. Designers kept looking for improvements.

Forsyth produced his first successful percussion lock in 1805.

Alexander John Forsyth: Reverend and Gun Designer

When not presiding over his Presbyterian church, the **Reverend Alexander John Forsyth** of Belhelvie, Scotland (1769–1843), hunted wild fowl. To Forsyth's frustration, his quarry often startled at the puff of smoke that emerged from the priming pan of his flintlock long gun before it discharged.

The percussion-ignition system Forsythe devised to not scare off birds earned him a place in firearm history. The design relied on a small container, or "scent bottle," to hold explosive fulminate of mercury, a chemical that worked as a primer but did not release smoke. Forsyth continued to develop the idea, working on behalf of the British military, though he eventually was dismissed out of fear he would blow up the arsenal in London. Forsyth did not appear to hold a grudge. When he was approached by Napoleon Bonaparte to bring his innovation to France, the clergyman-inventor demurred.

Percussion Cap Guns

A HAMMER RELEASED AND CAUSED
THE POWDER TO LIGHT.

During the 19th century, gunmakers began to gravitate to the latest firing-mechanism technology, the hammer-fired percussion cap. In some cases, owners of matchlocks, wheellocks, and flintlocks had their guns retrofitted to incorporate the new device.

Ring lever rotated the eight-chamber cylinder.

Muzzle-loading barrel

▲ MILITARY MUSKET

Country: Great Britain

Date: circa 1833

Barrel Length: 38 1/2in

Caliber: .750

This gun was converted from a flintlock to percussion ignition system.

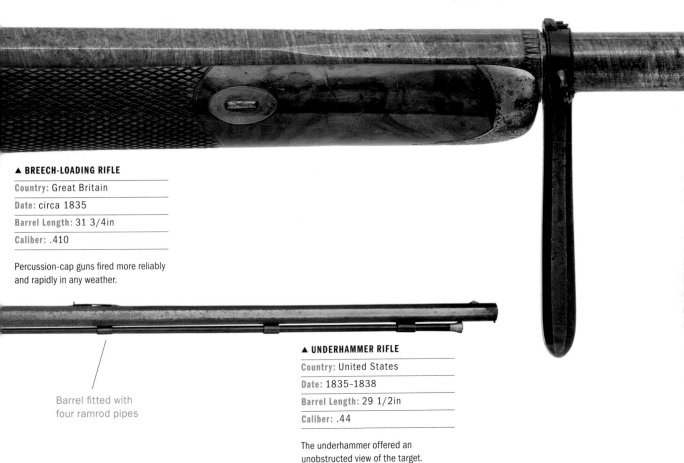

▲ BREECH-LOADING RIFLE

Country: Great Britain

Date: circa 1835

Barrel Length: 31 3/4in

Caliber: .410

Percussion-cap guns fired more reliably and rapidly in any weather.

Barrel fitted with four ramrod pipes

▲ UNDERHAMMER RIFLE

Country: United States

Date: 1835–1838

Barrel Length: 29 1/2in

Caliber: .44

The underhammer offered an unobstructed view of the target.

▲ COLT MODEL 1 PATERSON RIFLE

Country: United States

Date: 1837–1838

Barrel Length: 32in

Caliber: .36

The U.S. Army bought 50 of the first 200 Colt Model 1 Paterson rifles.

Percussion Cap Guns

▲ TARGET RIFLE

Country: United States

Date: mid 19th century

Barrel Length: 44 1/4in

Caliber: .52

This rifle was highly prized by
Native Americans and fur traders.

▲ PERCUSSION CAMEL GUN

Country: Afghanistan

Date: circa 1850

This type of gun was widely used in
the Middle East and North Africa.

▶ HARPER'S FERRY CARBINE

Country: United States

Date: 1857

Barrel Length: 33in

Caliber: .58

The Virginia armory that made this rifled musket was captured by the Confederacy in 1861.

FULL VIEW

▲ BREECH-LOADING DOUBLE-BARRELLED SHOTGUN

Country: France

Date: 1833

Barrel Length: 25 3/5in

Caliber: .66

This gun was primarily for hunting.

◀ AMERICAN BUGGY RIFLE

Country: United States

Date: circa 1835

Barrel Length: 28in

Caliber: .42

The Vermont-made barrel was designed to fit under a carriage seat.

Repeating Firearms

SMALL POCKET PISTOLS COULD FIRE A NUMBER OF TIMES BEFORE RELOADING.

At the same time that percussion-cap guns began appearing in the market, inventors moved to design weapons that could fire a number of shots before reloading. In 1837, a Massachusetts gunsmith named Ethan Allen (no relation to the Revolutionary War figure) patented a handgun that featured multiple rotating barrels, dubbed the "pepperbox" because it looked like a household pepper grinder. London gunsmiths Allen & Thurber produced a double-action pepperbox with four to six barrels that was a favorite feature among British gun owners.

Then there was Henry Deringer. Deringer (his famous Derringer pistol came to be spelled with two *r*'s) gained renown for large-caliber, short-barreled pistols that still used the flintlock action popular at the time, though he eventually integrated percussion-cap devices into his weapons. He also made muzzle-loading single-shot guns, as well as double-barreled versions with an over-under design. Easily concealable, the .41 caliber Derringer pistol could do lethal damage at close range. The gun's most notorious owner, John Wilkes Booth, used one to assassinate President Abraham Lincoln at Ford's Theater in Washington, D.C., on April 15, 1865.

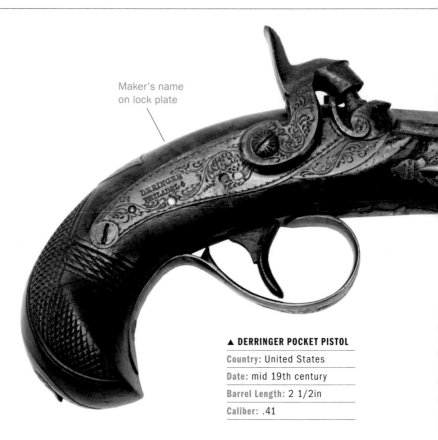

Maker's name on lock plate

▲ DERRINGER POCKET PISTOL

Country: United States

Date: mid 19th century

Barrel Length: 2 1/2in

Caliber: .41

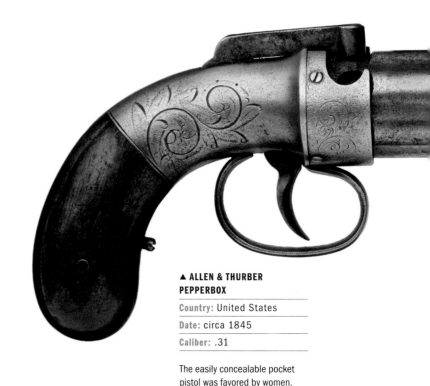

▲ ALLEN & THURBER PEPPERBOX

Country: United States

Date: circa 1845

Caliber: .31

The easily concealable pocket pistol was favored by women.

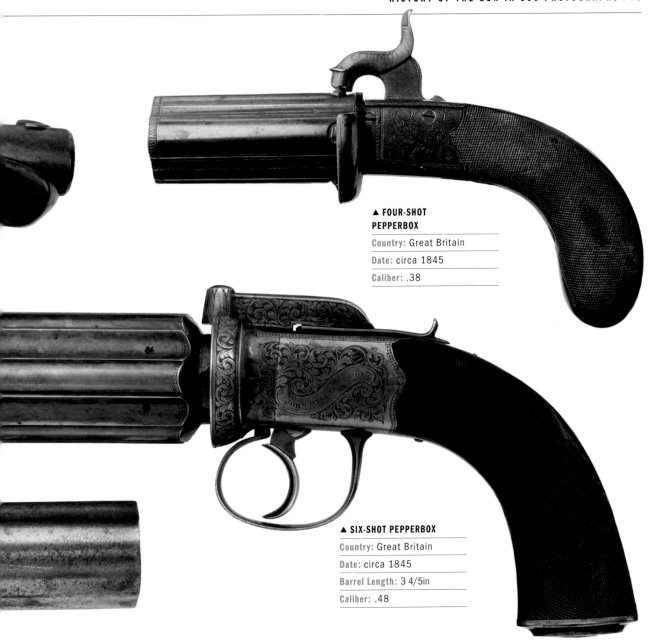

▲ **FOUR-SHOT PEPPERBOX**

Country: Great Britain

Date: circa 1845

Caliber: .38

▲ **SIX-SHOT PEPPERBOX**

Country: Great Britain

Date: circa 1845

Barrel Length: 3 4/5in

Caliber: .48

Exploiting Deringer's Designs

Henry Deringer (1786–1868) earned fame and fortune for his eponymous handgun but failed to fully protect his design with proper patents. As a result, imitators knocked off his ingenious guns, sometimes adding Deringer's name for the appearance of authenticity. Thanks to lucrative contracts with the military, including an agreement to make weapons sold by the government to Native American tribes, Deringer nevertheless became wealthy over the course of his long life.

1851 American-made Navy model with one-piece, walnut-finished grip

Samuel Colt:
A Life Defined by Firearms

A POPULAR SAYING IN THE OLD WEST HONORED THE GUNMAKER: "GOD MAY HAVE CREATED ALL MEN EQUAL, BUT SAM COLT MADE THEM SO."

Growing up in Hartford, Connecticut, Samuel Colt (1814–1862) inherited an old flintlock pistol carried by his maternal grandfather, an officer in the Continental Army during the Revolutionary War. The pistol became his prized possession and helped shape his view on life.

Colt's father, a farmer-turned-businessman, put Sam to work in a family-owned textile plant, but the young man grew restless, and in 1830, at the age of 15, he shipped out as a seaman's apprentice. It was during this period that Colt got the idea for a repeating firearm whose cylinder revolved, wheel-like, around the barrel.

Some accounts say the concept came to him as a result of studying the operation of the ship captain's wheel; others say that he got the idea from the capstan used to raise an anchor. Firearm historian Chuck Wills has written that Colt may have observed a flintlock revolver used by British troops in India and decided to

update it—a more prosaic discovery tale, but one that has the ring of plausibility.

A Defining Voyage

Colt himself pointed to a voyage aboard a brig called the *Corvo,* en route to Calcutta, as the beginning. At the time, existing multibarrel pepperbox designs required the shooter to rotate the barrels manually and estimate the proper cylinder-to-barrel alignment by eye. While at sea on the *Corvo,* Colt carved a model from scrap wood of a multibarrel revolver that would allow the shooter to rotate the cylinder by simultaneously cocking the hammer. The design also included a moving cylinder with multiple "charge holes" (five or six depending on the model) that aligned with the gun's barrel, thanks to recesses in the cylinder mating to a bolt in the gun's frame. When Colt returned to the United States in 1832, he set out to turn his wooden prototype into an actual firearm suitable

for civilians and soldiers alike.

Though Colt was determined to make a great gun and create the first true firearm factory, his progress was slow. His father, who financed some early production, withdrew his support after the first pistol Colt designed blew up when fired. To raise money, Colt took to the road as a "medicine man," performing demonstrations of the effects of nitrous oxide, or laughing gas. He called himself "the Celebrated Dr. Coult of New York, London, and Calcutta" and branched out from quasi-scientific quackery to ersatz mysticism, honing his confidence and marketing patter. With money saved from his road show, Colt hired professional gunsmiths from Baltimore to continue work on his ideas about firearms, primary among them a revolver with a single fixed barrel and a rotating cylinder.

The idea was not completely new. Boston inventor Elisha Collier already had introduced a flintlock revolver with a single fixed barrel.

Samuel Colt was expelled from an elite Massachusetts academy by age 15, but he had an agile mind. Fascinated with all things mechanical, he became an innovative gunmaker.

Colt's first sale—a .36-caliber repeating rifle—was made in 1836 in this Paterson, New Jersey, factory.

But Colt added a percussion-firing hammer mechanism and linked it to the cylinder's movement, eliminating the need to rotate the cylinder manually. To ensure his contribution was recognized both in Britain and in the United States, Colt applied for a patent for the design first in 1835 in London and only subsequently in his homeland. The following year the U.S. Patent Office granted him a pair of patents for a "revolving gun" and related mechanisms for a breech-loading weapon he called the Colt Paterson, a reference to his relocated workshop in Paterson, New Jersey, an early American manufacturing center.

A Setback and Detour

Colt wined and dined government officials he hoped would buy his new gun, but the U.S. Army and state militias showed little interest. With tepid sales and his backers refusing to sink more into the business, the Colt enterprise collapsed financially in 1843. The Paterson plant was sold off, and for the moment Colt found himself out of the gun business.

He turned to other inventions. He designed a tar-coated copper telegraph wire that Samuel Morse used to run communication lines beneath rivers and lakes. Colt also tried to sell the U.S. Navy an underwater mine for destroying enemy ships. The mine proved capable of blowing up a moving vessel, but in the early 1840s skeptical lawmakers in Washington scrapped his idea as an "un-Christian" method of warfare. (In later years,

THE COLT WALKER

Sam Colt's operation made relatively few of the original Colt Walkers, and in time the famous revolvers became museum pieces. Today, they are sought-after rarities among firearm collectors. In the 21st century, Colt Walkers have changed hands in private sales for nearly $1 million apiece.

◄ **WALKER PERCUSSION REVOLVER**

Country: United States	
Date: 1847	
Barrel Length: 9in	
Caliber: .44	

The cylinder was stamped with a fight scene between Texas Rangers and Native Americans.

With an effective shooting range of up to 100 yards, the Walker was one of the most powerful handguns of its era.

the destructive power of sea and land mines overshadowed any such religious scruples.)

As Colt cast around for products he could sell profitably, he settled on ammunition packaging. It was a time when ball and powder were packed together into a paper "cartridge" that ran into the age-old problem of rain. Colt replaced paper with a thin tinfoil that protected powder against moisture and didn't leave behind as much residue after firing. The U.S. Army tested and eventually began to acquire Colt's cartridges for use in infantry muskets. Colt's tinfoil solution was a midway step between paper cartridges and the metallic cartridges that would dominate the ammunition market by the late 19th century.

A Door Opens

But Colt was still intent on getting back into the gun business and saw a chance with Captain Samuel Walker of the Texas Rangers. Walker, it turned out, had acquired a small number of Colt's original revolvers and distributed them to members of the mounted Rangers for use during the Seminole Indian Wars in Florida in the late 1830s and early 1840s. Armed with Colt's invention, a 15-man unit under Walker's command had defeated a force of 70 Comanche warriors during a separate clash in Texas—or at least that was the story that Captain Walker told.

Eager to acquire more of Colt's revolvers for use in the Mexican-American War, Walker traveled to New York in January 1847 to meet with the firearm entrepreneur. Together they agreed on a tweaked design to accommodate six rounds instead of five, allow for easier reloading, and pack enough punch to kill a man (or a horse) at close range with one shot. With Walker's order for 1,000 guns, Colt's firearm business finally had a product, the single-action Colt Walker Model 1847, and the commercial foundation it needed.

Although Captain Walker was killed in combat shortly after receiving two of his namesake pistols, profits from the Colt Walker

Women were initially assigned the dangerous task of loading gunpowder into cartridges.

Model 1847, combined with a loan from a banker cousin, allowed Colt to open Colt's Patent Fire-Arms Manufacturing Company in Hartford. Soon the name Colt would become synonymous with revolver.

Colt had realized his goal of applying modern manufacturing techniques to producing guns. The new factory churned out standardized, machine-tooled, interchangeable parts that could be assembled swiftly by employees who weren't trained gunsmiths. The approach kept costs down and reduced the likelihood of product defects. It also gave Colt a platform: He enjoyed demonstrating the benefits of assembly-line manufacturing by taking apart a

group of his revolvers, scrambling the pieces, and showing how they could be put back together into reliable firearms.

As America expanded westward, Colt was poised to take advantage. He promoted his firearms as ideal for soldiers fighting Mexicans or Native Americans, and for civilian settlers defending themselves. In 1850, generals Sam Houston and Thomas Jefferson Rusk lobbied President James Polk at Colt's behest to adopt the Hartford-made revolvers as standard-issue sidearms for the U.S. Army.

"Colt's repeating arms are the most efficient weapons in the world and the only weapon which has

enabled the frontiersman to defeat the mounted Indian in his own peculiar mode of warfare," Rusk testified in language that Colt likely helped draft.

Stirring Consumer Interest

Colt's opportunism was legend. To impress potential buyers, Colt had himself named a lieutenant colonel in the Connecticut state militia and encouraged people to refer to him as "Colonel Colt." At the conclusion of the Mexican-American War, he sent salesmen to Mexico and marketed his guns to his own country's former foe. During the Civil War, he sold arms to both sides.

Teddy Roosevelt and his Rough Riders posed atop San Juan Hill in 1898.

Workers stand outside Colt's Hartford armory in 1876.

◄ **Colt SAA**

Country: United States

Date: circa 1898

Barrel Length: 5 1/2in

Caliber: .45

This revolver was carried up San Juan Hill by Rough Rider Louis Bishop.

When traditionalists invoked history, he stressed the "new and improved," a phrase historians credit him with coining. To stir consumer interest, he continually introduced slightly altered models with patriotic-sounding names. In what may have been the earliest use of product placement, Colt commissioned the western artist George Catlin to make a series of paintings of heroic scenes showing Colt firearms used against fierce Indians, deadly outlaws, and ferocious wild animals. Colt also paid a magazine to run a 29-page illustrated article depicting life and operations within his Hartford plant.

Colt died of gout in 1862, but his manufacturing plant thrived during the Civil War. In 1873, Colt's Manufacturing introduced the .44 Colt Single Action Army (SAA) Model, a hugely popular handgun that spawned several widely sold civilian models. Still made in replica today the Single Action Army became known as "the Peacemaker" and as "the gun that won the West."

In 1877, Colt's Manufacturing sought to capitalize on its association with the West by coming out with a version called the Colt Frontier Six Shooter. American soldiers carried the SAA during the domestic Indian Wars and the 1898 Spanish-American War, during which Teddy Roosevelt's Rough Riders took San Juan Hill armed with a .45-caliber variant called the Artillery Model.

Though the successor to Colt's Manufacturing has experienced financial challenges in recent years, Sam Colt's influence surpassed the 400,000 weapons his factory produced during his lifetime. Numerous rivals imitated his designs. His marketing genius transformed the firearm in America from a utilitarian military tool into a representation of national identity and technological supremacy. As much as any other person, he linked guns to the American ideals of individualism and self-reliance.

EYE ON THE PRIZE

Samuel Colt's career was defined by vision, some bad decisions, and savvy, ahead-of-his-time marketing.

1833 After his first attempt at producing a commercial revolver failed, Colt reinvented himself as a traveling medicine man and mystic.

1835–36 The entrepreneur obtained patents for his designs in the United States and Britain.

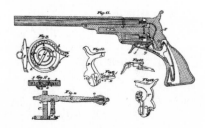

1847 Captain Sam Walker of the Texas Rangers committed to buy 1,000 Colt weapons. With the order and a timely loan, Colt opened Colt's Patent Fire-Arms Manufacturing Company in Hartford, Connecticut.

1820   1830   1840

1834 Colt used money saved from his road show to hire gunsmiths to execute his ideas, founding Patent Arms Manufacturing in Paterson, New Jersey.

1843 Without sufficient buyers, Colt was forced to close his plant in New Jersey.

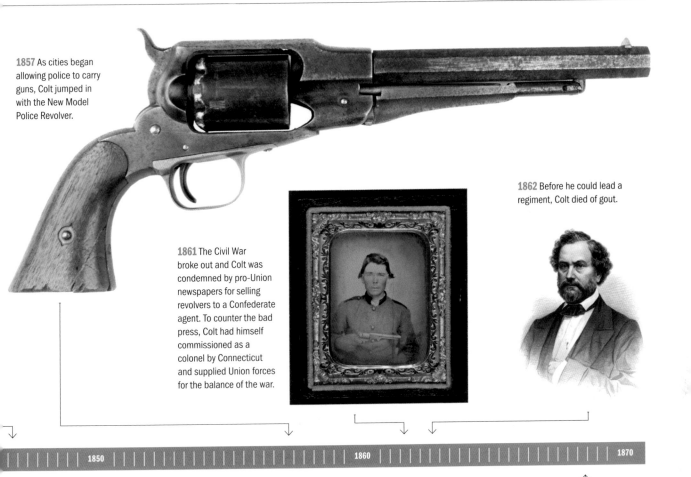

1857 As cities began allowing police to carry guns, Colt jumped in with the New Model Police Revolver.

1861 The Civil War broke out and Colt was condemned by pro-Union newspapers for selling revolvers to a Confederate agent. To counter the bad press, Colt had himself commissioned as a colonel by Connecticut and supplied Union forces for the balance of the war.

1862 Before he could lead a regiment, Colt died of gout.

| | | 1850 | | | | | | | | | | | | | 1860 | | | | | | | | | | | | | | 1870 | |

1853 Colt opened a factory near the Thames River in London but refused to tweak his models to reflect British taste. The factory closed three years later.

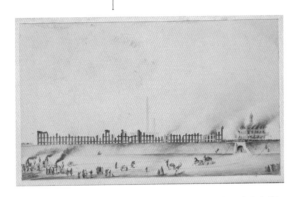

1864 The Colt factory in Hartford was engulfed in a fire. Though Colt did not feel the need to insure his building, after he died in 1862, his widow Elizabeth did. Following the fire, Elizabeth used the procceds from the policy to rebuild the facility on the same site.

Early Colt Models

BARRELS NO LONGER HAD TO
BE PRIMED SEPARATELY.

The development of the percussion cap enabled Samuel Colt to design his first revolver, a multishot weapon that automatically rotated the cylinder with the simple action of the hammer. The advantage of the new design was the chambers no longer had to be primed separately, but instead came into firing position ready to use. The design's major drawback was that there was no mechanism to lock the barrel group at the moment of discharge.

▼ **1851 LONDON NAVY REVOLVER**

Country: Great Britain

Date: mid 1850s

Barrel Length: 7 1/2in

Caliber: .36

An ad of the era touted the gun's popularity with the British military.

FULL VIEW

The loading lever is used to drive the bullets into the chamber.

◄ WHITNEYVILLE HARTFORD DRAGOON

Country: United States

Date: circa 1848

Barrel Length: 9in

Caliber: .44

Approximately 7,000 of these dragoons were manufactured.

▲ NO. 2 PATERSON BELT MODEL

Country: United States

Date: circa 1837–1840

A folding trigger remained invisible until the hammer was cocked. The model came in barrel lengths ranging from 2 1/2in to 5 1/2in and two calibers, .31 and .34.

Cylinder stamped with Colt's four-horse-head trademark

To speed up production at the Colt factory, superintendent Elisha Root created a rifling machine that cut grooves into four barrels at once.

Later Colt Models

TRENDSETTING GUNS WITH
LONG-LASTING INFLUENCE.

Though Elisha Collier introduced the flintlock revolver with a single priming pan, Colt's design advanced the revolver by linking the cylinder to the firing mechanism. As Colt's weapons evolved, they were considered safe, reliable, and powerful. Colt's factory in Hartford was the first firearm plant to take advantage of mass production and interchangeable parts—earmarks of the Industrial Revolution. Colt guns continued to be influential during and well after the Civil War.

▼ COLT 3rd MODEL DRAGOON

Country: United States

Date: circa 1851–1861

Barrel Length: 7 1/2in

Caliber: .44

Shoulder stock could be removed to convert rifle into a pistol.

▲ SINGLE ACTION ARMY MODEL

Country: United States

Date: 1873

Barrel Length: varying

Colt's most popular hand gun ever, the Single Action Army Model remains in production today.

Ten thousand of these dragoons were shipped to the front lines during the Indian Wars and the Civil War.

Walnut grip

▲ NAVY DOUBLE ACTION MODEL

Country: United States

Date: 1889

Barrel Length: 6in

Caliber: .38

The Navy bought 5,000 Colt 1889 revolvers. All but 363 were returned to the company for conversion to upgrade to the 1895 cylinder and locking system.

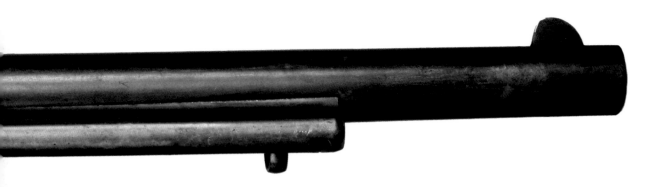

Brass trigger guard

▲ 1861 NAVY MODEL

Country: United States

Date: 1861

Barrel Length: 7 1/2in

Caliber: .36

Of the 38,000 1861 Navy Colts produced, this is one of the few that remain.

Ergonomic shape facilitated fast hammer cocking.

The Peacemaker

"THE GUN THAT WON THE WEST" DEBUTED IN 1873,
MORE THAN A DECADE AFTER SAMUEL COLT'S DEATH.

The 1873 Colt Single Action Army Model is the most copied gun in the world. Though the lines of the new models remain remarkably true to those made 143 years ago, "the Peacemaker" has been offered in more than 30 different calibers, several barrel lengths, and a variety of stock designs. In 1916 General George S. Patton Jr. ordered a sterling-silver plated SAA with inlaid ivory grips engraved with his initials. A few months later he used it in a shoot-out with Pancho Villa's bodyguards.

Designed for the U.S. military, the Single Action Army Model was the standard service revolver until 1892.

The gun originally cost $17 but now runs more than $1,700.

Colt: A Cinema Idol

The Academy Award–winning movie *High Noon* (1952) starred Gary Cooper as Will Kane, a small-town marshal who wants to turn in his badge and live peacefully with his new bride, Amy, a Quaker pacifist played by Grace Kelly. No such luck, of course, as Kane must confront a killer returning to seek revenge.

In addition to Cooper and Kelly, the other main star of the movie was the Peacemaker, Samuel Colt's six-shot Single Action Army revolver, perhaps the most famous firearm of the Hollywood Western. Kane and Deputy Harvey Pell (Lloyd Bridges) carried the 5 1/2–inch-barrel Single Action Artillery Model, also known as the .45-caliber Long Colt. The slightly smaller 4 3/4–inch-barrel version of the revolver turned up in the hands of Kane's antagonist, the villainous Frank Miller (Ian MacDonald).

Known as the Civilian or Quick-Draw model, the more compact variation also saw action courtesy of Amy Kane. When her brave husband's life is in danger, the Quaker frontierswoman sets aside her religious beliefs and fires off a few rounds of her own with a Peacemaker.

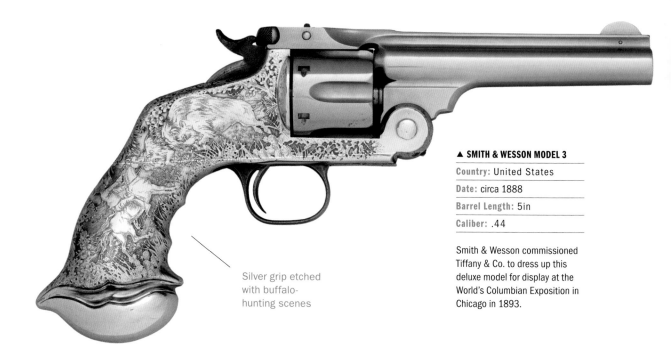

▲ SMITH & WESSON MODEL 3

Country: United States

Date: circa 1888

Barrel Length: 5in

Caliber: .44

Smith & Wesson commissioned Tiffany & Co. to dress up this deluxe model for display at the World's Columbian Exposition in Chicago in 1893.

Silver grip etched with buffalo-hunting scenes

The Rivals: Smith & Wesson

COLT'S COMPETITORS BECAME FAMOUS FOR "THE MOST POWERFUL HANDGUN IN THE WORLD."

Horace Smith and Daniel Wesson grew up in the nascent New England gun industry. Smith (1808–1893) worked at the federal armory in his native Massachusetts. Wesson (1825–1896), born in the same state, apprenticed with his older brother, Edwin, a leading gunsmith in the region. Smith and Wesson began working together in the 1850s in Connecticut, where they produced a repeating rifle that fired metallic cartridges containing the primer, powder, and bullet.

Like Samuel Colt, Smith and Wesson failed in their initial business venture but didn't give up. They sold their operation to Oliver Winchester, a shirtmaker who moved into the gun trade, then in 1856 reestablished their company. In fact, one of their early breaks came courtesy of a mistake made by Colt.

The better-known Colt fired an employee, Rollin White, who'd devised and proposed manufacturing an improved cylinder. White defected to Smith & Wesson, who developed a new metallic cartridge suited to White's "bore-through" cylinder design. Smith & Wesson continued with other innovations. In 1857, the

company introduced a .22 model that could be loaded more quickly than comparable handguns made by Colt. They followed that with a larger .32 version adopted by some units on the Union side of the Civil War.

Although they operated in Colt's long shadow, Smith & Wesson continued to introduce highly regarded handguns, such as the Model 3 Revolver (1870) and the .38 Model 1910 Military and Police. In 1935, the company introduced the powerful .357 Model 27 Registered Magnum, which became a standard for Federal Bureau of Investigation agents. During World War II, General George Patton at various times carried an ivory-handled Smith & Wesson .357 and a similarly decorated Colt Peacemaker. Patton referred to the Model 27 as his "killing gun."

Large frame to
handle powerful
magnum cartridge

▲ SMITH & WESSON MODEL 29

Country: United States

Date: 1960

Barrel Length: 6 1/2in

Caliber: .44

At the time this six-shooter was introduced, some owners found the handgun almost too power-ful. It "costarred" in the *Dirty Harry* films, which boosted sales.

Star of the Silver Screen

In later years, Hollywood elevated one Smith & Wesson handgun above all others: the .44 six-shot Magnum Model 29, introduced in 1955 and available in a variety of barrel lengths. In 1971, Clint Eastwood, playing Inspector "Dirty Harry" Callahan, pointed the enormous revolver at a criminal suspect as he uttered the ultimate tough-guy soliloquy: "I know what you're thinking: 'Did he fire six shots or only five?' But to tell the truth, in all this excitement, I've kinda lost track myself. But being as this is a .44 Magnum, the most powerful handgun in the world, and would blow your head clean off, you've got to ask yourself one question: 'Do I feel lucky?' Well, do ya, punk?" Sales of "the most powerful handgun in the world" soared.

Robert Adams' Double Action Revolver

While Colt's Manufacturing dominated handgun innovation and production in the mid and late 1800s, others offered competing models and made important advances. At London's Great Exhibition of 1851, the world's fair of its day, the British gunsmith Robert Adams (1809–1870) introduced the "double action" revolver which allowed the user to cock and fire with a single pull of the trigger, instead of cocking the hammer separately before firing, as Colt's design required. Some users struggled with Adams' heavier trigger, so he improved and reintroduced a new version, known as the Beaumont-Adams, for the Crimean War of 1854–1855. Some double-action Adams handguns saw action in the U.S. Civil War of the 1860s, but the double-action guns were handmade and far more expensive than Colt's single-action products, which were simpler, less prone to malfunction, and seen as more appropriate for the rough-and-tumble conditions of the American battlefield and frontier.

A Wave of Copycats

SAMUEL COLT'S DESIGNS WERE SO POPULAR, THEY SPAWNED NUMEROUS IMITATORS.

Few gunmakers copied Colt's earliest designs because they were so complex, but as his revolvers caught on, counterfeiters and copycats began capitalizing on his innovation. Uninformed buyers could easily mistake the fakes and some Belgian makers even stamped their wares with Colt's name. To protect his interests, Colt had his lawyer issue a notice to major arms dealers in the United States.

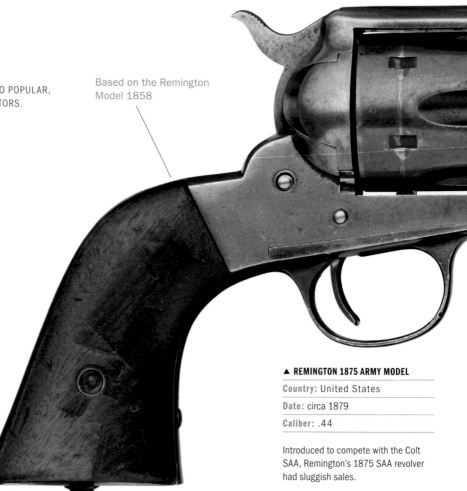

Based on the Remington Model 1858

▲ **REMINGTON 1875 ARMY MODEL**

Country: United States

Date: circa 1879

Caliber: .44

Introduced to compete with the Colt SAA, Remington's 1875 SAA revolver had sluggish sales.

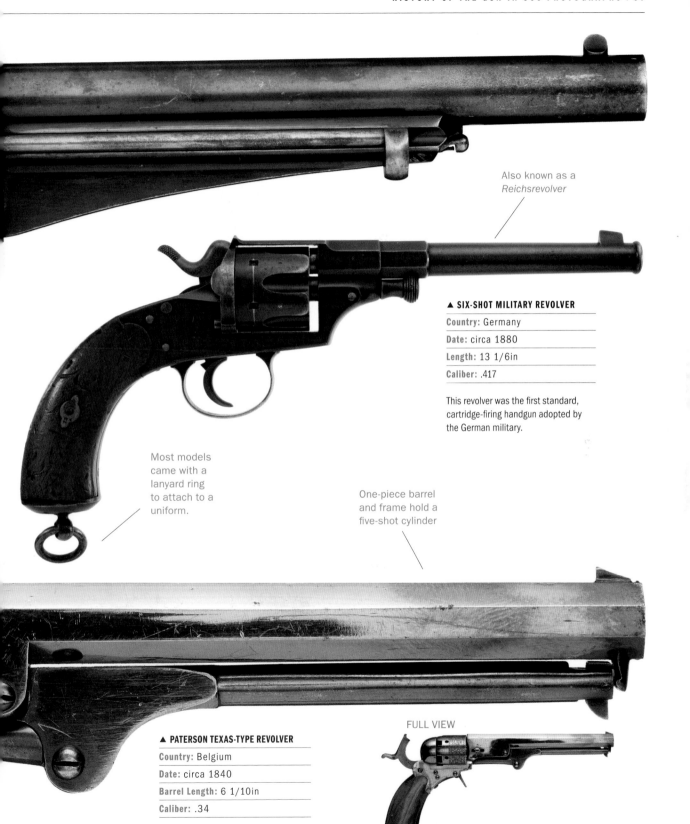

Also known as a
Reichsrevolver

▲ SIX-SHOT MILITARY REVOLVER

Country: Germany

Date: circa 1880

Length: 13 1/6in

Caliber: .417

This revolver was the first standard,
cartridge-firing handgun adopted by
the German military.

Most models
came with a
lanyard ring
to attach to a
uniform.

One-piece barrel
and frame hold a
five-shot cylinder

FULL VIEW

▲ PATERSON TEXAS-TYPE REVOLVER

Country: Belgium

Date: circa 1840

Barrel Length: 6 1/10in

Caliber: .34

6

THE CIVIL WAR AND THE RISE OF THE RIFLE

AMERICA'S BLOODY CONFLICT SPAWNED A NUMBER OF NEW WEAPONS, INCLUDING
THE SPRINGFIELD MODEL 1861 RIFLED MUSKET, PRECURSOR TO THE MODERN RIFLE.

In 1861, after the Civil War began, Union soldiers posed with bayoneted Springfields.

Polished-iron lock plate
and hammer

Oil-finished
walnut stock from
muzzle to butt

▲ 1861 MODEL SPRINGFIELD
RIFLE-MUSKET

Country: United States

Date: 1862

Barrel Length: 40in

Caliber: .58

Made at the Springfield Armory
in Massachusetts, this percussion weapon was widely used
throughout the Civl War. The
Springfield pictured above was
test fired but never issued.

A New Course for Weaponry

FEDERAL ARSENALS WERE ABLE TO PRODUCE BETTER LONG
GUNS AND REVOLVERS IN FAR GREATER VOLUME THAN
FACILITIES IN THE LIGHTLY INDUSTRIALIZED SOUTH.

The American Civil War inspired advances in firearms that in turn redefined armed conflict and reshaped American society. Referred to as the first truly "modern war," because of its brutal tactics and industrial-scale carnage, the clash between North and South saw the introduction and initial widespread use of breech-loading infantry firearms, repeating rifles, and rudimentary rapid-fire guns. Though disease and infection were the war's most insidious killers, more effective weapons also contributed to a combined death toll of some 700,000—more fatalities than in all other American wars combined. Firearm innovations associated with the Civil War set patterns that continued during the late-19th-century westward expansion of European-descended American settlers and

contributed to the slaughter of indigenous Native Americans.

The Union and Confederacy both entered the war unprepared to arm massive military operations, but the North rapidly gained a devastating advantage by using its superior industrial resources to produce weapons. Northern government arsenals, such as the one in Springfield, Massachusetts, and numerous other factories in New

More effective weapons contributed to a combined death toll of some 700,000.

England turned out long guns and revolvers of better quality—and in far greater volumes—than facilities in the lightly industrialized South.

The Union's Advantage

Still, it took a while for the North to gear up. In the first years of the war, many Union troops went into battle with antiquated .69–caliber flintlock muskets. Gradually, many of these old long guns were overhauled with percussion-cap firing systems. The North gained a distinct lead in the arms race when the Springfield Armory began churning out the Springfield Model 1861 rifled musket, a reliable weapon that came as close as any to serving as a standard-issue firearm for Union forces. Smaller factories and workshops across the North also made the Springfield 1861 under license arrangements.

A Union soldier posed with his nine-pound, .58-caliber Springfield.

▶ **REMINGTON NEW ARMY MODEL**

Country: United States

Date: circa 1864

Length: 13 3/4in

Caliber: .44

This six-shot revolver debuted about two years after the Colt 1860 Army. The Colt, which had early military contracts, dominated sales.

Forged steel barrel

Equipped with a bayonet, the Springfield weighed more than nine pounds and measured 58 inches, about the height of a typical soldier of the era. Although unwieldy by modern standards because of its size, the rifled Springfield musket proved far more accurate than its smoothbore predecessors. It fired a lead bullet, typically .58 caliber, and had an effective range of 200 yards. In recognition that even men of ordinary skill could actually aim the Springfield and hope to hit their target at some distance, Northern manufacturers began adding rear sights to Springfields, which further improved accuracy.

Union quartermasters issued ammunition that made the standard Springfield 1861 more deadly. Known as the Minié ball, after its French inventor, Claude Minié, the heavy bullet expanded as it traveled down the barrel, resulting in a tighter fit in the rifle grooves, and more rotation. Swifter rotation translated into steadier flight and greater precision.

All of these improvements made infantry units, even those manned by raw recruits, far more capable of inflicting death and destruction. Rather than charging across open fields, riflemen could establish defensive positions behind natural or man-made cover, firing several

rounds a minute with far more effect. Commanders on both sides, however, were slow to absorb the potential advantage of "digging in" defensively, and that led to many battles, particularly during the first half of the Civil War, in which unwitting soldiers charged in large numbers only to be mowed down by increasingly accurate rifle fire.

The Union enjoyed a further edge by exploiting the next generation of long guns: breech-loading and repeating rifles and carbines designed by gunsmiths such as Benjamin Henry, Christian Sharps, and Christopher Spencer. Rather than stuffing ammunition down the

Octagonal barrel with loading lever that compressed the bullet and powder into each of the cylinder's chambers

Spencer's new design included a tubular magazine in the buttstock, holding seven rounds.

▼ SPENCER LEVER ACTION CARBINE

Country:	United States
Date:	mid 1860s
Barrel Length:	22in
Caliber:	.52

John Wilkes Booth was captured and killed with a seven-shot Spencer carbine in his hand.

Claude-Etienne Minié: Designing a Better Bullet

Officer Claude-Etienne Minié (1804–1879) fought for France in colonial campaigns in Africa before turning his attention in the late 1840s to designing a bullet that later became known as the Minié ball.

Fired from a rifled barrel, Minié's cylindrical projectile had a conical point and resulted in noticeably improved accuracy. It featured an iron cup inserted in the hollow base of the bullet; when fired, the cup moved forward, expanding the base for a snug fit against the grooves of the rifling. In recognition of Minié's contribution, the French government awarded the officer a generous bonus and a position at the prestigious Vincennes military academy. He retired from the French army in 1858 with the rank of colonel and later served as a military adviser in Egypt and migrated to the United States, where he worked in a supervisory capacity at the Remington Arms Company.

barrel, an awkward, centuries-old procedure, a soldier with a breech-loader inserted his bullet into a chamber that was part of the rear portion of the barrel. Breech-loading weapons were particularly useful to cavalrymen who struggled with old-fashioned muzzle-loaders.

The Spencer carbine, introduced in 1860, featured both breech-loading and repeat firing. The rifle came equipped with a tubular "magazine," or ammunition container, located in its stock, which could hold seven .56-caliber copper-jacketed cartridges. The Spencer was the first repeat-fire carbine to be officially adopted by a major army; the Union bought more

than 100,000, which were mostly issued to elite infantry and cavalry units.

With the advent of more accurate rifles and carbines, long-distance sniping became a more common tactic. Both sides in the conflict formed specialized platoons of marksmen, the best known of which was Berdan's Sharpshooters, a Union outfit named for its commander, Hiram Berdan. The term sharpshooter may well have referred to the particular gun that many of Berdan's men carried: a breech-loading rifle designed by Christian Sharps, who began his career in the 1830s at the Harper's Ferry Arsenal in what's now West Virginia.

Guns of the North

IN THE FIRST YEARS OF THE WAR, SOME UNION FORCES CARRIED OLD FLINTLOCK MUSKETS.

Though the North was more heavily industrialized than the south, Union soldiers still were forced to scrambled to find guns for battle. Some brought their own long guns from home, but in time, the Springfield Armory began creating the Model 1861 rifled musket, and other small weaponmakers stepped up to produce the gun under a license arrangement.

Federal and state governments hired Colt to make more than 100,000 1861 muskets.

Brass trigger guard, patch box, and butt plate

Six-shot cylinder

▲ ALFRED P. JENKS & SON MODEL 1861 PERCUSSION RIFLED MUSKET

Country: United States

Date: 1861

Length: 40in

Caliber: .58

▲ REMINGTON-BEALS NAVY

Country: United States

Date: 1861–1863

Barrel Length: 7 1/2in

Caliber: .36

This was Remington's first military revolver.

**▲ COLT MODEL 1861
RIFLED MUSKET**

Country: United States

Date: 1865

Barrel Length: 40in

Caliber: .58

▼ HARPER'S FERRY MODEL 1841

Country: United States

Date: circa 1841

Barrel Length: 33in

Caliber: .54

Dubbed the "Mississippi rifle," for the U.S. regiment that prevailed in the Mexican-American War.

Alfred Jenks was one of 21 U.S. contractors making weapons for the North.

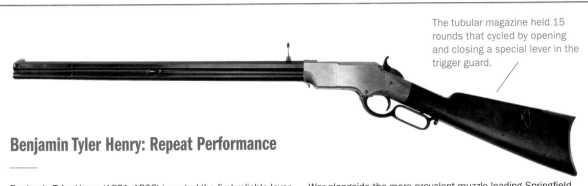

The tubular magazine held 15 rounds that cycled by opening and closing a special lever in the trigger guard.

Benjamin Tyler Henry: Repeat Performance

Benjamin Tyler Henry (1821–1898) invented the first reliable lever-action repeating rifle, widely known as the Henry rifle, and worked for several legendary figures in the 19th-century firearms industry.

In the 1850s, he helped design a rifle called the Volitional Repeater for entrepreneurs Horace Smith and Daniel Wesson of Smith & Wesson fame. He also worked for Oliver Winchester.

As the years passed, Henry became a respected designer in his own right and in 1860 obtained a patent on a .44–caliber breech-loading repeating rifle that saw action during the Civil War alongside the more prevalent muzzle-loading Springfield Model 1861. Later in the war, Henry and Winchester clashed over Henry's pay and the amount of recognition he received for his design work. Frustrated, Henry quit the Winchester Repeating Arms Company and was eclipsed by its owner, who had Henry's design overhauled and renamed the Winchester Model 1866. The .44–caliber Winchester 66 became one of the most widely used guns in the American West during the last third of the 19th century.

Portrait of a Union

CAPTURING BATTLEFIELD ACTION WAS ALMOST IMPOSSIBLE FOR CIVIL WAR
PHOTOGRAPHERS, BUT SOLDIERS OFTEN POSED WITH THEIR WEAPONS.

The Civil War became the first conflict in history to be thoroughly recorded in photographs. Because the technology was new, it was difficult to capture movement, and photographing battlefield action was almost impossible. Photographers turned to still subjects, and hundreds of soldiers headed off to war after posing for portraits so their loved ones would have a record.

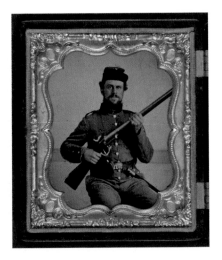

Hiram Berdan: Marksman and Leader

AN INVENTOR RECRUITED ELITE UNION
SOLDIERS TO JOIN THE SHARPSHOOTERS.

Hiram Berdan (1823–1893), a New York engineer and inventor, was a renowned marksman and guiding force behind the U.S. Volunteer Sharpshooter Regiments during the Civil War. He was the inventor of the Berdan repeating rifle, the Berdan centerfire primer, and numerous other weapons and accessories.

Recruits in Colonel Berdan's units had to pass marksmanship tests, wore distinctive green uniforms, and carried repeating rifles and carbines designed by Christian Sharps. The men frequently were deployed to skirmish and harass Confederate forces from a distance, and fought at some of the most important battles of the war, including the Second Battle of Bull Run, Shepherdstown, and Chancellorsville. At the Battle of Gettysburg, Berdan's Sharpshooters helped slow Confederate assaults on Devil's Den and the Peach Orchard. After the war, Berdan returned to military inventing, and his creations included a submarine gunboat and a torpedo boat.

New York sharpshooter Hiram Berdan scoured the Northern states to find proven marksmen who specialized in scouting, skirmishing, and sniping.

A Berdan recruit cradles his Sharps rifle. Touted as "superior to any other arm in the service," it cost $45, nearly four times as much as the Army-issue Springfield.

The 1859 breech-loading .52 Sharps could fire up to ten rounds a minute.

Christian Sharps: Aim High

As a boy, Christian Sharps (1810–1874) apprenticed to a New Jersey gunsmith and in the 1830s worked as a laborer at the Harper's Ferry Arsenal in Virginia. Not content to be a hired hand, Sharps taught himself about breech-loading rifle designs and became an expert on the use of interchangeable parts. By the 1840s, he had refined what became known as the Sharps rifle, a gun known for its long-range accuracy, and received a U.S. patent for it in 1848.

Sharps' Model 1849 became the first breech-loading rifle to gain wide acceptance. A smaller, lighter carbine version was especially popular with the Union Army. Jealous of the rapid, accurate firing capacity of the Sharps carbine, the South tried to reverse-engineer the gun, but Confederate knockoffs functioned poorly. After the war, Sharps continued designing firearms and launched a trout-farming business in Connecticut before dying of tuberculosis in 1874.

Christopher Spencer: Weapon Entrepreneur

Born in Connecticut, Christopher Spencer (1833–1922) learned about making guns in Samuel Colt's Hartford factory. He went on to invent a repeating rifle that bore his name and was one of the first lever-action long guns widely used in the United States.

Like so many other weapon entrepreneurs of the era, Spencer struggled at first as a businessman. Hoping to get a contract to produce rifles for the Union, he embarked on an audacious lobbying effort. Striding into the wartime White House one day in August 1863, Spencer made his way past sentries and gained access to the office of President Abraham Lincoln. This led to a subsequent meeting during which Spencer and Lincoln, joined by Secretary of War Edwin Stanton, tested Spencer's creation. The presidential party relocated to the nearby National Mall, where Lincoln personally fired the rifle and declared it worthy.

The Union began ordering Spencer rifles and carbines, and none other than General Ulysses S. Grant declared them "the best breech-loading arms available." After the war, many veterans kept their rifles, and Spencer arms became popular among Western settlers. The proliferation of military surplus dampened sales for the Spencer Repeating Rifle Company, however, and the company slipped into insolvency in 1868. The following year, its assets were acquired by another prominent figure in the gun trade, Oliver Winchester.

De Lamater,

Spencer reentered the arms business in Windsor, Connecticut, in the 1880s. His workers produced slide-action repeating rifles.

FULL VIEW

Tubular magazine
in the butt held
seven rim-fire
cartridges.

▲ SPENCER MODEL 1860 RIFLE

Country: United States

Date: 1863

Barrel Length: 30in

Caliber: .52

The Spencer rifle and carbine
were both highly valued on the
battlefield.

Adjustable rear sight

Rifled barrel for pistol bullets

Smoothbore barrel for buckshot

Percussion lock

Rifle sling attachment

Arming a Breakaway Nation

UNTIL THE UNION NAVY'S BLOCKADES CUT SUPPLY LINES FROM EUROPE,
THE SOUTH IMPORTED ARMS FROM SUCH SOURCES AS ENGLAND AND AUSTRIA.

In an imbalance that played an important role in the war's outcome, the Confederacy lacked the workshops and factories that powered the Union Army. The South scrambled to arm itself creatively —by building knockoffs of successful guns used by the North or scavenging them from battlefields. In 1861, for example, Confederate forces captured the federal arsenal at Harper's Ferry in what was then Virginia. That raid yielded an immediate boon—the armory's store of rifles—and also a trove of tools and machinery that Southern military officials used to establish smaller factories elsewhere.

The secessionist states also turned to Europe for help. Though the British government officially maintained neutrality and the Royal Arsenal at Enfield was not permitted to supply the Confederacy, small private factories were eager for the business and sold the Confederacy hundreds of thousands of Enfield .577-caliber rifled muskets. Austria, too, provided arms, selling a limited number of Model 1854 Infanteriegewehr, or infantry rifles.

Yet the South never came anywhere close to matching the manufacturing capacity of the North, and the guns they did make were often inferior. When makers tried to imitate breech-loading Union weapons like the Sharps carbine, their mechanically inferior version, called the "Rich-

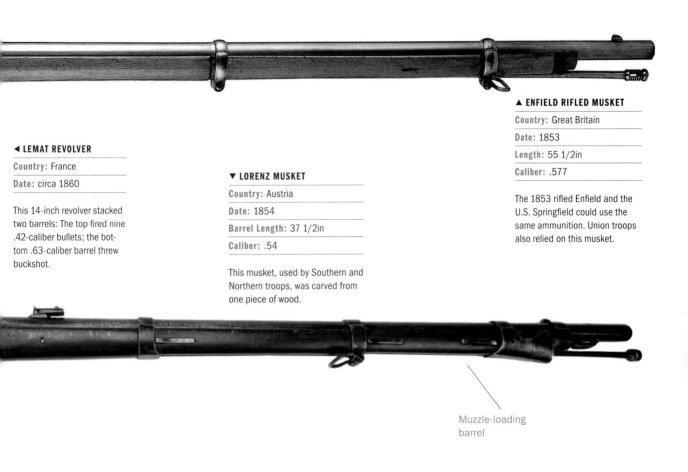

◄ LEMAT REVOLVER

Country: France

Date: circa 1860

This 14-inch revolver stacked two barrels: The top fired nine .42-caliber bullets; the bottom .63-caliber barrel threw buckshot.

▼ LORENZ MUSKET

Country: Austria

Date: 1854

Barrel Length: 37 1/2in

Caliber: .54

This musket, used by Southern and Northern troops, was carved from one piece of wood.

▲ ENFIELD RIFLED MUSKET

Country: Great Britain

Date: 1853

Length: 55 1/2in

Caliber: .577

The 1853 rifled Enfield and the U.S. Springfield could use the same ammunition. Union troops also relied on this musket.

Muzzle-loading barrel

mond Sharps," failed frequently in battle. Confederate general Robert E. Lee disparaged the gun as "so defective as to be demoralizing to our men." The South was further disadvantaged in the arms race once Union blockades of Southern ports cut supply lines from Europe.

In early-model guns, shooters measured out the right amount of powder propellant and placed it in the barrel along with a bullet (known as a ball) and some wadding to secure the powder and projectile in place and put a percussion cap on the nipple for the hammer to strike. This system was referred to as cap-and-ball, and was

used in the first revolvers designed by Colt in the 1830s. The new revolvers had the advantage of allowing shooters to fire off a succession of five or six shots but still required the gunman to laboriously reload each chamber with loose powder and a lead bullet and then place a percussion cap on the nipple of each chamber.

At about the same time, European gunsmiths were developing a more efficient shooting system that relied on self-contained paper cartridges with a metal base that contained primer, powder, and bullet in one unit. By 1846, Benjamin Houllier of Paris had created a cartridge pressed

from copper or brass—all metal and a single piece. In 1860, the American Benjamin Tyler Henry improved on the same basic design by adding a hollow rim that contained the chemical primer. Such "rim fire" cartridges tended to be delicate and subject to accidental discharge. Still, rim-fire ammunition enabled repeating weapons, such as the Spencer rifle, to fire a dozen rounds in a minute. Hiram Berdan later developed a one-piece brass case that contained primer in a percussion cap at the center of the cartridge's base, a more stable and reliable design that became standard for weapons of all sorts.

As Union forces approached Richmond, Virginia, Confederate soldiers were ordered to torch anything of military value, including the state armory.

Southern Industry

FACTORIES OPENED ACROSS THE CONFEDERACY, AS MAKERS
SOUGHT TO CATCH UP WITH THEIR NORTHERN FOES.

A largely agrarian society, the American South suffered a terrible disadvantage when it came to arms manufacturing. Southern gunmaking operations were small and inefficient compared to their Northern rivals. In New Orleans, for example, Ferdinand W.C. Cook and his brother, Francis, both English citizens, opened a rifle factory on Canal Street in June 1861. They initially supplied Alabama militias and then won a substantial contract from the Confederacy for 30,000 arms. But the fall of New Orleans in 1862 forced them to relocate to Athens, Georgia. The state of Tennessee operated armories at Columbia, Memphis, Nashville, Gallatin, and Pulaski that converted flintlock muskets to percussion-cap weapons. The Pulaski and Gallatin facilities made new carbines and rifles.

In Memphis, Leech & Rigdon, also known as Memphis Novelty Works, made imitation Colt revolvers of dubious quality, which

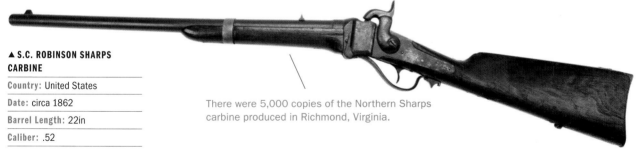

▲ **S.C. ROBINSON SHARPS CARBINE**

Country: United States

Date: circa 1862

Barrel Length: 22in

Caliber: .52

There were 5,000 copies of the Northern Sharps carbine produced in Richmond, Virginia.

they sold to the Confederacy. The Shakanoosa Arms Company of Dickson, Alabama, manufactured so-called Mississippi rifles (Model 1841) and bayonets. It had to relocate and ended up in Dawson, Georgia, in 1864. Some of the larger Confederate arms operations were captured federal facilities. In April

Leech & Rigdon, also known as Memphis Novelty Works, made imitation Colt revolvers of dubious quality.

1861, North Carolina forces seized the U.S. arsenal at Fayetteville. This victory added some 36,000 muskets and rifles to Confederate stores. Machinery captured from the takeover of the Harper's Ferry Arsenal was shipped to Fayetteville, which soon began rifle production of its own.

Confederate Firearms

PRODUCTION PROBLEMS PROVED
HARD TO OVERCOME FOR THE SOUTH.

The South not only lacked factories to make guns when the war broke out, but it did not have a ready supply of crucial materials such as steel. Sometimes iron was substituted, and sometimes brass—thanks in part to churches which donated their brass bells "for the Cause"—which was melted down for use in pistol frames.

▶ RICHMOND MUSKET

Country:	United States
Date:	1861
Length:	56in
Caliber:	.577

The Richmond Armory also cobbled together Springfield knockoffs with equipment raided from Harper's Ferry.

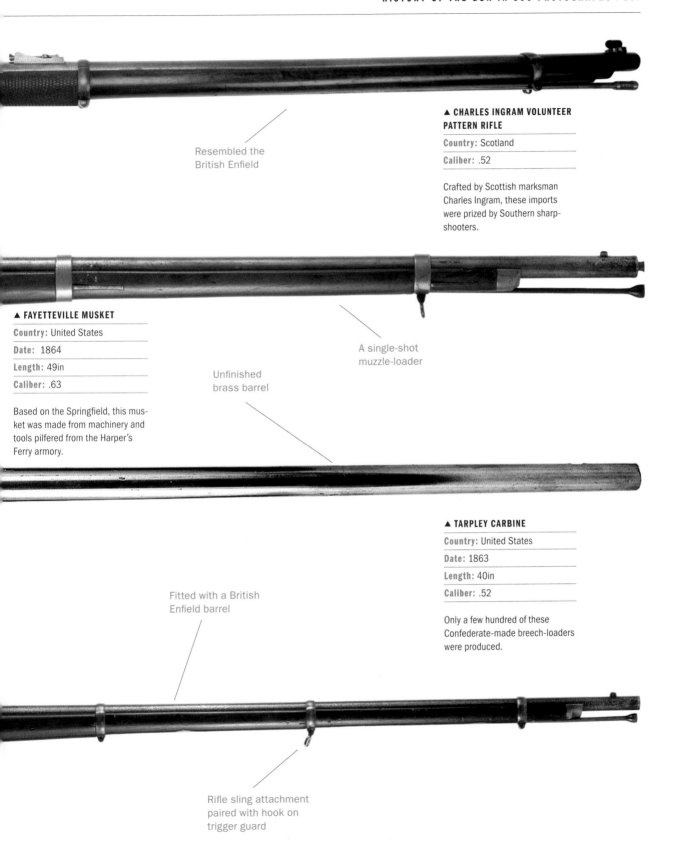

Resembled the
British Enfield

▲ CHARLES INGRAM VOLUNTEER PATTERN RIFLE

Country: Scotland

Caliber: .52

Crafted by Scottish marksman Charles Ingram, these imports were prized by Southern sharp-shooters.

▲ FAYETTEVILLE MUSKET

Country: United States

Date: 1864

Length: 49in

Caliber: .63

Based on the Springfield, this musket was made from machinery and tools pilfered from the Harper's Ferry armory.

A single-shot
muzzle-loader

Unfinished
brass barrel

▲ TARPLEY CARBINE

Country: United States

Date: 1863

Length: 40in

Caliber: .52

Only a few hundred of these Confederate-made breech-loaders were produced.

Fitted with a British
Enfield barrel

Rifle sling attachment
paired with hook on
trigger guard

Portrait of the South

LIKE THEIR BRETHREN IN THE NORTH, CONFEDERATE SOLDIERS
POSED WITH THE WEAPONS THEY USED ON THE BATTLEFIELD.

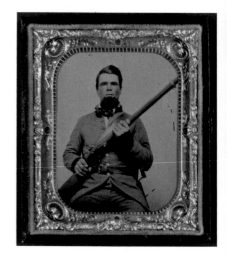

Photographic equipment and chemicals were harder to come by in the South, but some Confederate photographers still managed to record the war. George S. Cook of South Carolina, who studied under famous Northern photographer Mathew Brady, moved to Charleston just before the war began and captured early images of the Battle of Fort Sumter. Portraits also were popular with soldiers.

KILLING FIELDS

Breech-loading infantry firearms, repeating rifles, and rudimentary rapid-fire guns led to a staggering death toll during the Civil War.

1861 February: Confederate States of American formed; Jefferson Davis sworn in as president.

1861 July: The Battle of First Manassas (Bull Run), Virginia, claimed 4,900 casualties.

1862 September: The Battle of Antietam Creek, Sharpsburg, Maryland, totaled 23,000 casualties in a single day.

1861 | **1862** | **1863**

1861 April: Confederate troops fired on Fort Sumter in Charleston Harbor, South Carolina. President Abraham Lincoln ordered a blockade of Confederate ports.

1862 August: The Battle of Second Manassas (Bull Run), Virginia, claimed 25,000 casualties.

1863 January: Lincoln signed the Emancipation Proclamation.

1863 July: The Battle of Gettysburg, Pennsylvania, had 51,000 casualties (below top) July 1 to 3. Seige of Vicksburg, Mississippi (bottom) had 50,000.

1864 November: Lincoln reelected.

1865 March: Battle of Petersburg, Virginia, (below, top). The Confederacy authorized the arming of slaves as rebel soldiers (bottom).

1864   1865   1866

1864 July: The Confederate raid on Washington, D.C., ended with 9,000 casualties; the battles for Atlanta had 20,000 casualties.

1865 April: Confederate General Robert E. Lee (above) surrendered at Appomattox Courthouse, Virginia. Five days later, Confederate sympathizer John Wilkes Booth (right) assassinated Lincoln in Washington, D.C.

PATENT MODEL OF THE GATLING GUN

Designed by Richard Gatling in 1862, this wooden patent prototype was 36 inches long, with six 11 1/2–inch barrels. An improved model was officially adopted by the U.S. ordnance department four years later.

The Birth of Rapid-Fire Weapons

HOPING TO REDUCE THE TOLL OF INFECTIONS, A NONPRACTICING PHYSICIAN CREATED A MORE EFFECIENT GUN.

Another innovation spurred by the Civil War was the rapid-fire gun, a precursor to the modern machinegun. Manually operated by means of a crank, these weapons had multiple barrels and were capable of unleashing 100 rounds a minute—assuming, of course, they didn't jam. Richard Gatling, an eccentric inventor and nonpracticing physician, introduced the best-known model in 1861. Gatling's original creation had six barrels and fired paper-wrapped cartridges. The action of the crank caused the barrels to revolve around a cylindrical shaft as cartridges dropped into place from above and were struck by the firing pin.

Union military leaders rejected the Gatling Gun in 1862 because they thought it was too heavy and complicated to operate. It didn't help the weapon's reputation that Gatling, who lived and worked in Indianapolis, was rumored to be a Confederate sympathizer because he had been born in North Carolina. Individual Union commanders bought a handful of Gatling Guns on their own, and the weapons played a role, albeit limited, during the Union siege of Petersburg, Virginia, in 1864.

Later 10-barrel Gatling variations fired metallic cartridges from a drum-shaped magazine at a rate of up to 1,000 rounds a minute. The U.S. Army used them to deadly effect in Cuba during the Spanish-American War of 1898.

RICHARD GATLING: FATAL FIRE

Inventor Richard Gatling (1818–1903) not only designed machines for planting rice and wheat, he transferred those concepts to the field of firearms, developing the precursor to the machinegun.

As the Civil War unfolded, Gatling noted that more men were dying from disease than weapon fire. He came up with the unusual notion that a rapid-fire gun would require fewer men to pull the trigger, reducing the toll of fatal infections. "If I could invent a machine—a gun—which could by its rapidity of fire, enable one man to do as much battle duty as a hundred... it would, to a large extent supersede the necessity of large armies," he wrote.

As it turned out, Gatling's gun did more to multiply death by bullet than to reduce fatalities attributable to disease. In 1870, he sold his patents for the machine to Colt.

7 | FIREARMS AND THE WILD WEST

TO CONQUER NEW TERRITORY AND BATTLE NATIVE AMERICANS, SETTLERS AND
CATTLEMEN RELIED ON WINCHESTERS, SHARPS, AND COLTS.

Photo. and copyright by Grabill, 1891,
Deadwood, S. D.

Buffalo Bill (far left), General Nelson Miles of the U.S. Army (center), and officers survey the aftermath of the December 29, 1890, Wounded Knee massacre that killed 300 Sioux men, women, and children.

Rear sight

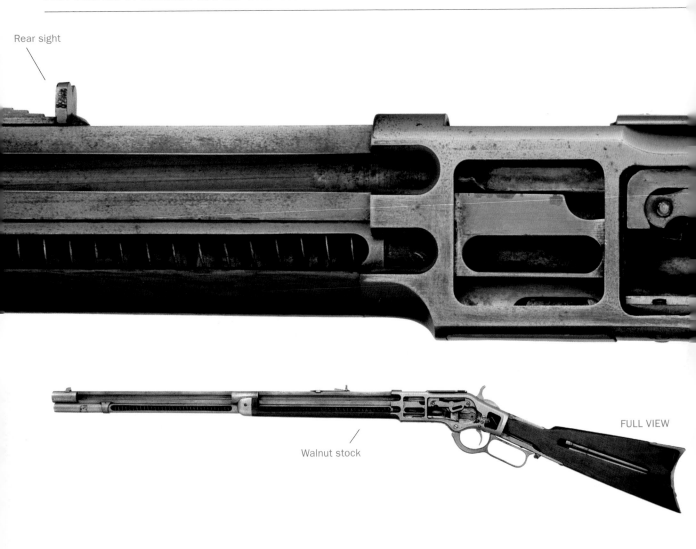

Walnut stock

FULL VIEW

The Role of Weapons in the Wild West

IN THE YEARS AFTER THE CIVIL WAR, CIVILIANS, SOLDIERS, AND OUTLAWS USED OLIVER WINCHESTER'S LEVER-ACTION RIFLES.

Cowboys and Indians, outlaws and marshals, federal troops and land-hungry settlers—all were characters of mythic proportion during the late-19th-century surge of population from East to West. In the sweep of imagination and in quite a bit of actual experience, guns played a central role in the era of the "Wild West."

It was the age of Colt six-shooters, Winchester lever-action repeaters, and Sharps rifles that could take down a charging bison with a single well-placed shot. A romantic attachment to firearms—and the violence they begat—was woven into American popular culture.

No man had a greater influence on the weaponry of the West than Oliver Winchester, an East Coast shirt manufacturer who diversified into the gun business by investing in the Volcanic Repeating Arms Company, a division of Smith & Wesson. When

Factory cutaway reveals a
15-round tubular magazine
under the barrel.

◀ **WINCHESTER MODEL 1873**

Country:	United States
Date:	circa 1873
Barrel Length:	24in
Caliber:	.44

Manufactured from 1873 to 1919, this
lever-action rifle also was made as a carbine and rifled musket. It competes with
the 1873 Colt Single Action Army .45 for
the title "the gun that won the West."

Combination
trigger guard and
firing lever

Winchester took control of Volcanic
in 1856, he changed its name to the
less evocative Winchester Repeating
Arms, and based it in New Haven,
Connecticut. Among his many
talented craftsmen, Winchester
employed Benjamin Tyler Henry,
designer of the lever-action repeating

Henry rifle, which saw action during
the Civil War.

After the Union prevailed,
Winchester introduced a series
of lever-action rifles that became
popular in the West among civilians,
soldiers, bandits, and lawmen.
The Winchester Model 1866, a

descendant of the Henry rifle
nicknamed "Yellow Boy" because
of the color of its brass receiver,
could hold 15 .44-caliber rim-fire
cartridges in its tubular magazine,
more than twice the seven-round
capacity of its famous predecessor.
Armed with that amount of

▲ **WINCHESTER MODEL 1895 CARBINE**

Country: United States

Date: late 19th century

Barrel Length: 22in

Caliber: .30

This rifle is chambered for a variety of military and hunting cartridges.

Military-style forearm

Straight grip on crescent-style buttstock

Brass frame and buttplate

▲ **WINCHESTER YELLOW BOY**

Country: United States

Date: 1866-1900

Caliber: .44

▲ **WINCHESTER MODEL 1873 LEVER-ACTION RIFLE**

Country: United States

Date: 1891

Barrel Length: 24in

Caliber: .44

Over 720,000 manufactured

firepower, the skilled gunman was a force to be reckoned with.

Winchester's subsequent Model 1873 discharged an even more effective center-fire cartridge, also .44 caliber, and became the most prominent rifle of the last quarter of the century. The weapon was so influential, it shared the honorific "the gun that won the West," with Sam Colt's Single Action Army revolver.

Other notable rifles of the Wild West era included the Sharps 1859 carbine, which was popular with scouts and hunters and even starred in some movies, like *True Grit* (1969) and *Valdez Is Coming* (1971). Some Sharps carbines incorporated a hand-cranked grinder in the gun's stock, a curious feature once thought to be a coffee mill but now assumed to be used for grinding wheat or corn. Buffalo hunters tended to prefer the Sharps .50 caliber—"the Big Fifty"—which supposedly could kill a bison at a distance of 200 yards.

Eliphalet Remington (1793–1861) of upstate New York designed a single-shot rifle bearing his name and manufactured by his family-owned company in the town of Ilion. Popular in the West in the 1860s and 1870s, durable Remington rifles were also purchased in large numbers by European governments. Over the generations, what became the Remington Arms Company branched out to manufacture typewriters, cash registers, and cutlery. But Remington continued to make firearms as well, and today, Remingtons are produced by a descendant company based in North Carolina.

Oliver Winchester: Empire Builder

A sharp-eyed businessman, Oliver Winchester (1810–1881) got into the gun business by snapping up a financially troubled division of Smith & Wesson, Volcanic Repeating Arms, and turning it into an eponymous firearm empire. During the Civil War, the Union Army bought some of the company's repeating Henry rifles for its troops, but conservative-minded military officials generally equipped infantrymen with single-shot weapons thought to be easier to use. Winchester's fortunes as a gunmaker improved after the war, when civilians moving west adopted repeating weapons such as the Winchester Model 1873 to battle Native Americans.

After Winchester died, ownership of his company passed to a son, William, who himself died shortly thereafter, a victim of tuberculosis. William's wife, Sarah, became convinced the family bore a curse cast by spirits of the legions killed over the decades with Winchester rifles. She moved to San Jose, California, and built a bizarre mansion, the Winchester Mystery House, a vast dwelling with 160 rooms, doors that opened on to walls, and stairways to nowhere. Sarah apparently thought she could hide there from hostile mystic forces seeking revenge against Oliver Winchester's heirs.

The house today is a tourist attraction and the Winchester brand remains alive, a reminder of the Old West, albeit in a license agreement with a Belgian-based group.

A statue in the garden at the Winchester Mystery House was installed to help appease spirits of Native Americans killed by Winchester guns.

Soldiers of the West

FRONTIER NEEDS DOMINATED AMERICAN MILITARY ACTION FOR
MOST OF THE 19TH CENTURY.

A soldier guarded South Dakota's Fort Lincoln, circa 1876.

Frontier soldiers laid out roads and helped advance railroads through the Great Plains. But their primary mission during the 19th century was to protect a tide of white settlers from the Native Americans they were displacing. Countless battles and hundreds of broken peace treaties finally led to two of the best known and most controversial frontier encounters: Lieutenant Colonel Custer's 1876 slaughter at Little Bighorn and the 1890 Sioux massacre at Wounded Knee.

A well-armed cavalier monitored Sioux who were being forced onto reservations in late 1890.

Soldiers with the Hotchkiss cannon used to attack Sioux at Wounded Knee in December 1890.

Soldiers flanked a Sioux warrior acquitted of killing a U.S. Army officer in 1891.

Infantrymen prepared for war with the Sioux in 1890.

Seventy U.S. Army scouts two weeks before the December 29, 1890, attack on the Sioux camp at Wounded Knee.

Country: Germany	
Date: 1890	
Barrel Length: 24in	

Double barrel

Buffalo Bill gave Oakley this 12-gauge shotgun during their 1889–1890 tour.

Annie Got Her Guns

A FEMALE SHARPSHOOTER AND ENTERTAINER MADE HER NAME IN BUFFALO BILL'S VARIETY SHOW.

Annie Oakley (Phoebe Ann Mosey, 1860–1926), a star of Buffalo Bill's Wild West show and one of the first Americans to truly deserve the title of celebrity, used a wide variety of rifles and shotguns to accomplish her feats of accuracy. Her first trick shot came at the age of eight, she recounted: "I saw a squirrel run down over the grass in front of the house, through the orchard, and stop on a fence to get a hickory nut." Oakley took down the family rifle and fired. "It was a wonderful shot, going right through the head from side to side," she remembered.

As an adult, Oakley delighted audiences with a rare .32-caliber, single-shot Remington-Beals rifle manufactured briefly in the late 1860s. She also used double-barrel shotguns made by Parker Brothers and Hibbard, as well as a Stevens Tip-up trick shot rifle. She dazzled crowds with her .22-caliber Marlin, obliterating an ace of hearts playing card nearly 40 feet away with 25 shots in just 27 seconds. When Oakley turned to revolvers, she relied on the best-known brands of the day: the Smith & Wesson Model 3 and various Colt handguns.

Checkered grip and
walnut buttstock

▲ REMINGTON-BEALS RIFLE

Country: United States

Date: circa 1866–1868

Caliber: .32

"When a man hits a target, they
call him a marksman," Oakley
once said. "When I hit a target,
they call it a trick. Never did like
that much."

▼ STEVENS-GOULD NO. 37

Country: United States

Date: 1890s

Barrel Length: 10in

Caliber: .22

Gold-plated,
mother-of-
pearl grip

Palm-size
pistol

▲ SMITH & WESSON MODEL 1

Country: United States

Date: 1881

Caliber: .22

The seven-shot Model 1 was the
company's first firearm.

The Other Side of the Law

WEAPONS USED BY BANDITS AND GANG MEMBERS LIKE JESSE JAMES AND BILLY THE KID WERE AS FAMOUS AS THEIR OWNERS.

Hard-rubber grips

Old West outlaws preyed on banks, trains, and stagecoaches. In off hours, they frequented saloons where gambling disputes and severe inebriation led to further gunplay. Jesse James, a former Confederate bushwhacker who formed a criminal gang with his brother Frank, used a distinctive .45-caliber Smith & Wesson Schofield revolver. Tom "Black Jack" Ketchum, an affiliate of the Hole-in-the-Wall gang, carried the most famous of the Old West revolvers, the Colt .45 Single Action Army. John Wesley Hardin also preferred a Colt, but his was a .41-caliber Model 1877 double-action revolver.

Billy the Kid (Henry McCarty), known for his mild demeanor when he wasn't murdering people, likewise carried the Colt .41, nicknamed "the Thunderer," as well as a Winchester Model 1873 rifle. The dapper train robber Butch Cassidy (Robert Leroy Parker) surrendered his Colt .45 Single Action Army to a sheriff in Utah as part of a failed bid for amnesty; when the deal fell through, he and his partner, Harry Alonzo Longabaugh, a.k.a. the Sundance Kid, returned to their life of crime using other Colt weapons and Winchester rifles—models 1873, 1894, and 1895.

▲ **SMITH & WESSON SCHOFIELD**

Country: United States

Date: late 1876

Barrel Length: 7in

Caliber: .45

Jesse James carried a Smith & Wesson Schofield.

◄ COLT THUNDERER

Country: United States

Date: circa 1879

Barrel Length: 4 1/2in

Caliber: .41

John Wesley Hardin used a six-shot, double-action Colt Thunderer to rob a high-end crap game in El Paso, Texas, in 1895.

Designed to be operated with one hand so a cavalry soldier could reload while riding his horse

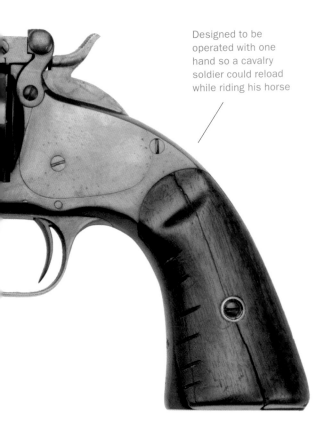

In this image of Billy the Kid, he carries a holstered Colt SAA and is leaning on his 1873 Winchester carbine.

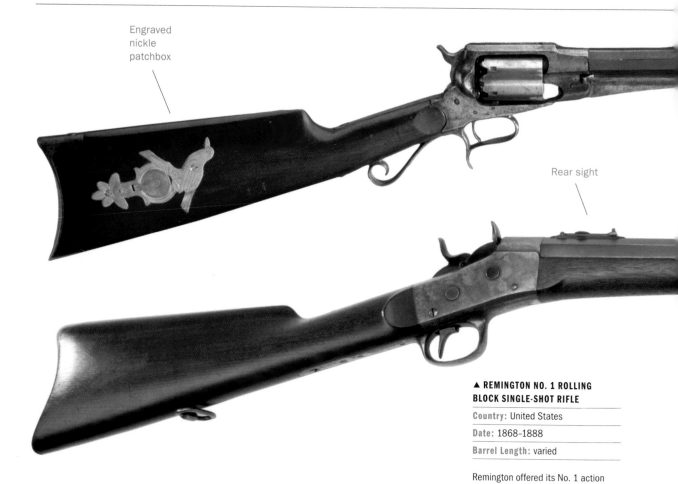

Engraved nickle patchbox

Rear sight

▲ **REMINGTON NO. 1 ROLLING BLOCK SINGLE-SHOT RIFLE**

Country: United States

Date: 1868–1888

Barrel Length: varied

Remington offered its No. 1 action rifle in more than 30 different calibers. It sold more than a million copies worldwide.

The Rule of Remington

THE CIVIL WAR HELPED SPUR THE GROWTH OF AN INFLUENTIAL FAMILY GUNMAKING BUSINESS.

An archetypal New England gunmaker, Eliphalet Remington (1793–1861) initially followed his father into the blacksmithing trade in rural upstate New York. At 23, the younger Remington bought a flintlock firing mechanism from a nearby gunsmith, fashioned a barrel to go with it, and produced his first rifle. The weapon worked well enough that he decided to manufacture rifles, forming E. Remington & Sons with his own offspring. Eliphalet and his son Philo produced the first successful cast-steel drilled rifle barrel made in the U.S.

The onset of the Civil War created demand for Remington's products, as it did for those of Colt, Sharps, and other highly regarded gunmakers. After the founder's death in 1861, what became known as Remington Repeating Arms Company and later just Remington Arms made guns for the Union in the Civil War and the U.S. military during World War I and World War II.

Eliphalet Remington

Octagonal barrel

▲ REMINGTON NEW MODEL PERCUSSION RIFLE

Country: United States

Date: circa 1865

Caliber: .36 and .44

Only about 1,000 of these New Model rifles were produced.

◄ REMINGTON NEW MODEL ARMY REVOLVER

Country: United States

Date: 1863–1875

Barrel Length: 8in

Caliber: .44

This military sidearm was sold commercially to civilians after the Civil War. "It never failed me," Buffalo Bill said of the revolver he used for 43 years.

The Remington Arms Company assembly room in 1917.

The plant, which once employed more than 17,000 people, closed in 1986.

Lakota chief Sitting Bull added star power to Cody's revue, but his duties were limited. He rode in the show's opening procession and sold autographs.

In the peak years of Buffalo Bill's Wild West show, the cast logged 341 performances in 132 cities within 200 days. By 1910, the cowboy showman had expanded the spectacle with performers from all over the world.

Buffalo Bill Cody: Bison Hunter and Showman

While Oliver Winchester manufactured the arms of the Old West, William Frederick "Buffalo Bill" Cody (1846–1917), bison hunter and showman, made guns a part of American culture and mythology. Born in Le Claire in what's now the state of Iowa, Cody moved with his family to the Kansas Territory and at the age of 14 became a rider for the Pony Express. He fought with the Union Army during the Civil War and served as a celebrated military scout during the long Indian Wars that followed. Cody also hunted bison, supposedly killing more than 4,000 in an 18-month period in the late 1860s—an example of the sort of excess

that almost drove the iconic animal to extinction by the late 19th century. Illustrating his flair for the romantic, Cody named his Springfield Model 1863 "Lucretia Borgia," after the notorious Italian noblewoman.

In 1883, he started Buffalo Bill's Wild West, a circuslike revue with a large cast of performers who traveled not only throughout the United States but across Europe as well. The show featured intricate presentations of horsemanship and shooting by uniformed U.S. military veterans, weather-worn cowboys, Indians in native garb, and colorfully costumed participants from as far away as Turkey and South America. For a time, Lakota chief Sitting Bull appeared with a group of his warriors. Annie Oakley and her husband, Frank Butler, demonstrated acrobatic sharpshooting with weapons made by Winchester, Remington, Colt, and Smith & Wesson, among many others. The show often ended with a lurid simulation of whooping Plains Indians attacking the humble cabin of a brave white settler family who would be rescued by heroic cowboys or federal soldiers. At the turn of the 20th century, Cody was probably the best-known show-business celebrity on earth and most recognizable ambassador of the United States.

Guns at Little Bighorn

THOUGH REPEATING RIFLES WERE AVAILABLE, SOLDIERS WERE
EQUIPPED WITH SINGLE-SHOT MODELS TO SAVE ON AMMUNITION.

The now politically incorrect term "cowboys and Indians" typically conjures the Wild West era. But it was far more common in the late 19th century for units of the U.S. Army to confront Native Americans in battles for territory and dominance—and militarily, the Plains Indians outwitted, outplanned, and outmaneuvered the cavalrymen. At the 1876 Battle of Little Bighorn, for example, a combined force of Lakota, Cheyenne, and Arapaho warriors vanquished 700 men under the command of George Armstrong Custer. Five of the dozen companies of the 7th U.S. Cavalry were wiped out, with 263 Army soldiers killed, including Custer. About 40 to 50 Native Americans are thought to have died in the confrontation.

A number of factors contributed to the debacle known as Custer's Last Stand. Custer ignored warnings from his scouts, his command was riven by internal rivalries, and most fatally, he divided his forces. The deployment of firearms also played a role.

Custer's cavalry troops went into battle with breech-loading, single-shot Springfield Model 1873 carbines and .45 caliber Colt 1873 Single Action Army revolvers. Repeating rifles designed by Henry, Spencer, and Winchester were all available at the time, but the post–Civil War U.S. Army's ordnance department stuck with a single-shot rifle as its standard, in part because the Springfield was relatively inexpensive to manufacture but also because they thought soldiers armed with single-shot weapons would be less likely to waste ammunition. Army officers were also following the lead of European militia, which generally avoided

Lieutenant Colonel George A. Custer and 262 7th Cavalry soldiers were outmanned and outgunned at the Battle of Little Bighorn in Montana in 1876.

repeating weapons. Custer rejected an offer to add rapid-fire Gatling Guns to his arsenal, telling an Army colleague that bulky wheeled Gatling Guns would "hamper our movements." The 7th Cavalry, a cocky Custer added, "can handle anything it meets."

The Little Bighorn Battlefield National Monument, with tributes to Native Americans and the 7th U.S. Cavalry.

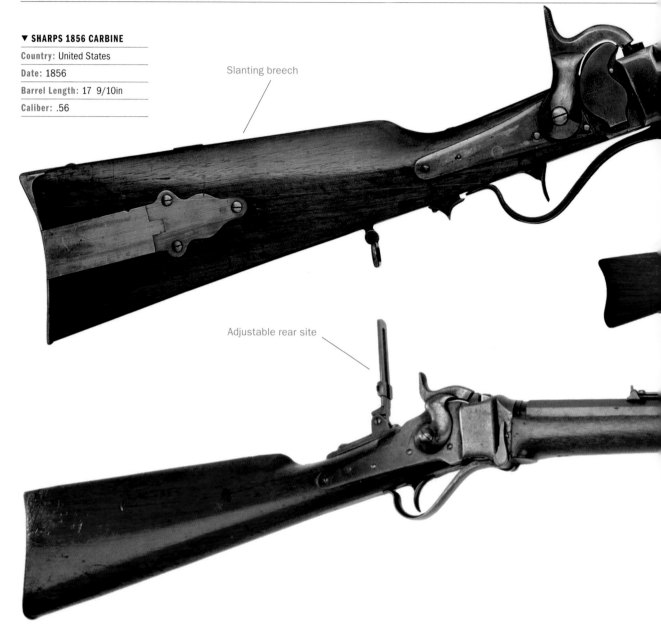

▼ SHARPS 1856 CARBINE

Country:	United States
Date:	1856
Barrel Length:	17 9/10in
Caliber:	.56

Slanting breech

Adjustable rear site

The several Indian groups came to the fight at Little Bighorn with an extraordinary array of weapons purchased and scavenged over time. Some of the Native Americans carried traditional bow and arrow, and when the dust settled, a number of Army dead resembled human pincushions. But the Native American warriors did far more damage with firearms. Hundreds of the mounted tribe members carried rifles and revolvers, including Henrys, Sharps, Winchesters, Remingtons, Smith & Wessons, and even British Enfields (the latter originally imported by the Confederate Army during the Civil War).

Historical accounts include the recollection of a Cheyenne warrior named Wooden Leg, who was armed with what he said was a "six shooter," probably a Colt revolver. White Cow Bull, an Oglala Lakota warrior, claimed to have a repeating rifle. All told, historians have found evidence of 62 Indian-owned .44-caliber Henry repeaters and 27 .50-caliber Sharps rifles. Survivors emphasized that the native warriors were able to fire more rounds more quickly than the confused men under Custer. "The Indians had

Classic cavalry carbine
of the Old West

▼ **SPRINGFIELD MODEL 1873**
"TRAPDOOR" RIFLE

Country: United States

Date: 1876

Barrel Length: 32 1/2in

Caliber: .45

Walnut forearm

▲ **SHARPS BIG 50 RIFLE**

Country: United States

Date: 1872

Caliber: .50

Up to 60 million bison were
killed in the latter half of the
19th century. Sharps .50-caliber
rifles added to the carnage.

Shooters could hit
a target more than
1,000 yards away.

Winchester rifles, and [the Army] column made a large target for them, and they were pumping bullets into it," recalled Major Marcus Reno.

For a supposedly crack cavalry unit, the U.S. 7th betrayed a distinct lack of skill with those weapons it did possess. Before Little Bighorn, the military allotted only 20 rounds per soldier for training. "Those were the good old days," one Army

Survivors reported that native warriors were able to fire more rounds more quickly than the confused troops under Custer.

veteran recalled of the 1870s. "Target practice was practically unknown."

In the end, of course, the Native American military prowess was not enough to defeat the Army and arriving settlers. Bison hunters exterminated their food supply, eventually starving tribes. With no immunity to European diseases, thousands more were killed by typhus and smallpox.

Butch Cassidy: Outlaw and Folk Hero

At the turn of the 20th century, Robert Leroy Parker (1866–1908), the bank and train robber better known as Butch Cassidy, teamed with Harry Alonzo Longabaugh, a.k.a. the Sundance Kid, in a long string of celebrated crimes.

During their careers, the felonious duo used a variety of weapons, but were most commonly linked to Colt revolvers and Winchester rifles— the standards of the Old West. In the 1890s, Cassidy and the Sundance Kid led the Wild Bunch, a gang that in 1899 robbed a Union Pacific train near Wilcox, Wyoming, leading to an extraordinary—and unsuccessful—manhunt. To avoid lawmen, Cassidy, the Sundance Kid, and the latter's lady friend, Etta Place, fled to Argentina and then Bolivia, where the two robbers are thought to have been shot and killed in 1908. Their exploits inspired the 1969 Western *Butch Cassidy and the Sundance Kid*, starring Paul Newman and Robert Redford.

In 2012, a Colt .45 Single Action Army revolver once owned by Cassidy was sold for $175,000 at an auction. According to legend, Cassidy surrendered the handgun, along with a Winchester rifle, in late 1899 or 1900 to a sheriff named Parley Christison in an abortive bid for amnesty.

Robert Leroy Parker (left) and his outlaw partner Harry Longabaugh, better known as Butch Cassidy and the Sundance Kid, were often portrayed as likable bandits.

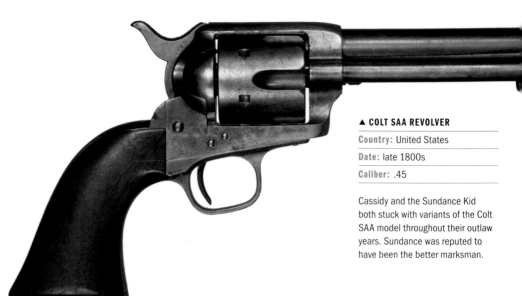

▲ COLT SAA REVOLVER

Country: United States

Date: late 1800s

Caliber: .45

Cassidy and the Sundance Kid both stuck with variants of the Colt SAA model throughout their outlaw years. Sundance was reputed to have been the better marksman.

After a $50,000 Union Pacific heist, Pinkerton agents ran the notorious duo out of the train-robbing business—and the country.

Paul Newman (left, as Cassidy) and Robert Redford (as Longabaugh) romanticized the notorious bandits in the 1969 film Butch Cassidy and the Sundance Kid.

SHOWDOWNS AND SHOOT-OUTS

High-octane gunfights were as much a part of the Old West as cowboys, wagon trains, buffalo hunters, and railroads.

1871 Abilene marshal "Wild Bill" Hickok tried to censor a painting in gambler Phil Coe's saloon of a bull with unusually large testicles; Coe was killed in the shoot-out that followed.

1874 Bison hunters including lawman Bat Masterson shot it out with Comanche at the Second Battle of Adobe Walls.

1876 After attacking a Sioux village in Montana Territory, Lt. Col. George Custer and the 7th U.S. Cavalry Regiment were massacred in the Battle of Little Bighorn.

1870		1875		1880

1873 U.S. Army forces collaborating with Apache scouts defeated Yavapai and Tonto Apache bands at the Battle of Turret Peak in Arizona.

1876 Sioux Chiefs Sitting Bull and Crazy Horse refused to leave the Black Hills of the Dakota Territory, leading to the Battle of Powder River.

1876 Wild Bill Hickok was shot and killed during a poker game in Deadwood, Dakota Territory.

1877 Claiming self-defense, Billy the Kid, 17, killed his first victim in a saloon fight in Fort Grant, Arizona.

1881 The Gunfight at the O.K. Corral, perhaps the most famous shoot-out of the Wild West, unfolded over a brief 30 seconds behind a saloon in Tombstone, Arizona.

1886 Geronimo surrendered and was taken into custody at Fort Grant, Arizona, symbolically ending the Apache Wars.

1890 The U.S. Cavalry killed 300 Sioux at Wounded Knee on the Pine Ridge Reservation in South Dakota.

1882: Hoping to collect a $10,000 reward, outlaw Bob Ford killed gang leader Jesse James (pictured).

1889 Butch Cassidy (front, right) knocked over his first bank, in Telluride, Colorado.

1892 Residents of Coffeyville, Kansas, shot and killed four members of the Dalton Gang after the outlaws tried to rob two banks in the town simultaneously.

8 | WORLD WAR I AND INDUSTRIALIZED WARFARE

THE GREAT WAR WAS DEFINED BY THE WEAPONS USED TO FIGHT IT,
FROM IMPROVED BOLT-ACTION RIFLES TO AUTOMATIC WEAPONS.

In the fall of 1918, during the Battle of Argonne Forest, a rain-soaked American machinegun crew advanced toward critical rail lines that supplied entrenched German troops.

bB-305

▼ SPRINGFIELD MODEL 1903

Country:	United States
Date:	circa 1903
Barrel Length:	24in
Caliber:	.30

For three decades, this was the
standard rifle for the U.S. military.

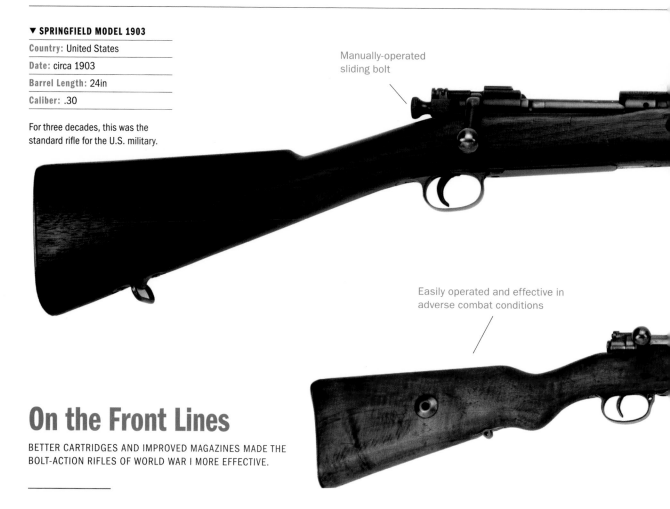

Manually-operated
sliding bolt

Easily operated and effective in
adverse combat conditions

On the Front Lines

BETTER CARTRIDGES AND IMPROVED MAGAZINES MADE THE
BOLT-ACTION RIFLES OF WORLD WAR I MORE EFFECTIVE.

Improved weaponry made World War I one of the deadliest military conflicts in history. More than 9 million combatants and an additional 7 million civilians lost their lives from July 1914 through November 1918 as a result of the global clash between the Allied powers—led by Britain, France, and later the United States—and the Central powers of Germany, Austria-Hungary, and the Ottoman Empire. Ordinary infantrymen on both sides went into battle with bolt-action, repeat-fire rifles, some designed in the 19th century. But as clouds of poison gas and salvos of artillery shells descended from above, the introduction of heavy machineguns helped make trench warfare far more terrifying and lethal.

A More Effective
Bolt-Action Rifle

Sturdy bolt-action rifles have a small handle, typically on the right-hand side of the weapon, which opens and closes the breech, or barrel. When the user manipulates the handle back and forth, the gun's bolt unlocks and the breech opens. If there is a spent cartridge case in the chamber, this action causes it to be ejected, making room for a new round.

Decades before the outbreak of World War I, the German state of Prussia introduced a single-shot bolt-action rifle designed by Johann Nicolaus von Dreyse, the son of a locksmith who traveled to Paris to study firearm production. Formally called the Zündnadelgewehr M 1841, Von Dreyse's creation became known as the "needle gun." Its needle-shaped firing pin contacted a primer cap incorporated into a paper cartridge that also contained the main powder charge and lead bullet. During the Franco-Prussian War (1870–1871), Prussian troops armed with the Zündnadelgewehr encountered French foes using their own, superior version of the single-shot bolt-action rifle, the chassepot,

One of the Springfield Armory's
legacy weapons

▼ MAUSER 98

Country: Germany

Date: 1916

Barrel Length: 29in

Caliber: 7.92mm

This was Germany's World War I
standard infantry rifle.

An Allied soldier charged across a barbed-wired battlefield on France's Western Front.

▲ DREYSE NEEDLE RIFLE

Country: Prussia	
Date: 1860s	
Caliber: .60	

Considered the first bolt-action breech-loader, the rifle used a long, thin pin to mechanically puncture the gun's paper cartridge to initiate firing.

Capable of shooting up to seven rounds per minute

Detachable 10-round magazine

which was named for its inventor, Antoine Chassepot.

By the early years of the 20th century, two improvements made the bolt-action rifles that would appear in World War I more effective. First, ammunition designers replaced paper-wrapped cartridges with factory-produced metal-jacketed cartridges containing primer, propellant and bullet. Less likely to explode prematurely, the self-contained metallic cartridges were loaded into the weapon not one at a time by hand, but from the second improvement: a magazine containing five or more rounds. Some rifles, such as the Swiss Vetterli, had a tubular magazine beneath the barrel; more commonly, bolt-action weapons had fixed or detachable box-shaped magazines.

A shooter could fire as swiftly as he could operate the bolt handle, ejecting an empty cartridge case and loading a fresh one from the magazine. Changing magazines took only seconds, allowing a skilled soldier to fire dozens of rounds in a minute.

The British armed infantrymen in World War I with the .303-caliber SMLE, which stood for Short Magazine Lee-Enfield. British troops referred to their sturdy SMLEs as "smellies." The comparable American weapon was the Springfield M1903. Unprepared for a major war and short on Springfield rifles, the U.S. military also adopted a version of the SMLE called the U.S. Rifle Model 1917, which was modified to accommodate American .30-'06 cartridges. The German equivalent was the 7.92mm Gewehr (rifle) Model 1898 and its smaller, lighter sibling, the Karabiner (carbine) 98, both designed by the Mauser brothers, Germany's premier turn-of-the-century gunsmiths.

▲ **SMLE (SHORT MAGAZINE LEE-ENFIELD)**

Country: Great Britain

Date: 1907

Barrel Length: 25 1/4in

Caliber: .30

The SMLE offered the fastest, most reliable firing capacity of its day.

James Paris Lee: Military Designer

James Paris Lee (1831–1904) was a Scottish-born gunsmith who relocated first to Canada and then to the United States; eventually his most important designs were adopted by the British military in World War I.

Lee built his first weapon from spare parts at the age of 12; the gun didn't actually work, but the young man had found his life's pursuit. After settling in Wisconsin, Lee obtained a small contract to make carbines for the Union during the Civil War. Later he invented a spring-loaded, column-fed magazine system for rifles that could accommodate either individual cartridges, loaded one at a time, or a "charger" device preloaded with five rounds (also known

as a "stripper clip"). Rifles incorporating Lee's magazine system were adopted by the U.S. Navy in the 1880s and later sold commercially as the Remington-Lee M1885 and Winchester-Lee M1895.

Lee's bolt-action, magazine-equipped designs soon attracted the attention of the British military. In 1907, three years after Lee had died, the Royal Small Arms Factory in Enfield began producing the SMLE, the standard-issue British infantry gun for World War I and for decades thereafter. With a detachable 10-round magazine or stripper clip, the SMLE allowed for such rapid fire that some German soldiers mistook Lee's creation for a machinegun.

THE GREAT WAR UNFOLDS

The sophisticated weapons used in the world's first global conflict lead to unprecedented bloodshed.

1916 February–December: The Battle of Verdun, the longest of the war, ended in a draw with one million casualties.

1914 June: Archduke Franz Ferdinand, heir to the throne of the Austro-Hungarian Empire, and his wife were assassinated with a Browning pistol in Sarajevo.

1914 July–August: Austria-Hungary declared war on Serbia; Russia, an ally of Serbia, mobilized; Germany declared war on Russia and then on France and Belgium; Britain declared war on Germany; Austria-Hungary declared war on Russia.

| 1914 | 1915 | 1916 |

1915 May: A German U-boat sank the *Lusitania,* killing 1,198 civilians, including 128 Americans.

1915 December: Allies withdrew from Gallipoli after a brutal nine-month battle for the Turkish peninsula.

1916 July–November: The Battle of the Somme resulted in another one million casualties with no Allied breakthrough.

1917 November: Bolshevik socialists led by Vladimir Lenin overthrew the provisional Russian government of Alexander Kerensky, leading to an armistice with Germany.

1917 April: President Wilson asked Congress for a declaration of war against Germany.

1918 April: British and Australian forces stopped the German advance near Amiens.

1918 July: German troops began to desert in large numbers; former czar Nicholas II and his family were killed by the Bolsheviks carrying Browning and Mauser handguns.

1917 | 1918 | 1919

1917 July: The American Expeditionary Force landed in France.

1918 September: Allied troops broke through the German Hindenburg line.

1918 November: Kaiser Wilhelm II abdicated; the German republic was founded, and the next day (11/11/18) Germany and the Allies signed an armistice.

European Rifles

THE BOLT-ACTION RIFLE CAME OF AGE ON THE
BATTLEFIELDS OF THE WESTERN FRONT.

Bolt-action rifles were the most common infantry weapons used during the Great War. For the British, the favored model was the Lee-Enfield .303, a gun that had been used by the army since 1902. It was robust and reliable, and a well-trained soldier could fire dozens of rounds a minute with the gun. German infantry relied on the Gewehr 98, a bolt-action better known in the United States as the Mauser 98. It was longer than the Lee-Enfield and also well made, but at nine pounds and 49 inches, it was unwieldy for use in the trenches of the Western Front.

Fixed five-shot box magazine

Five-round magazine

▲ K98A

Country: Germany

Date: 1916

Barrel Length: 24in

Caliber: 7.92mm

Made to replace the larger M98, this carbine was issued to mountain units and front-line troops.

▲ ENFIELD NO. 3 MARK 1 RIFLE

Country: Great Britain

Date: circa 1914

The paired-down Enfield quickened the pace of production.

◄ MOSIN-NAGANT M1891

Country: Russia

Date: 1902

Barrel Length: 32.5

Caliber: 7.62mm

Russian factories could not meet demand for this weapon, so manufacturing was outsourced to the United States, Britain, and other countries.

▲ CACANO 1891

Country: Italy

Date: 1900

Barrel Length: 30in

Caliber: 6.5mm

The manufacturer used an Italian bolt paired with with a Mannlicher magazine.

Produced in rifle and carbine form

Wilhelm and Paul Mauser: Brothers in Arms

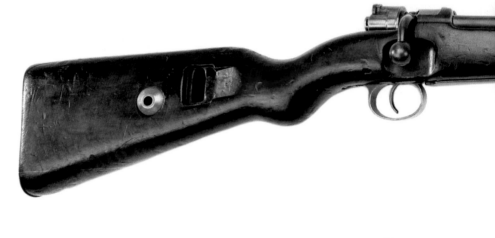

The Mausers, Wilhelm (1834–1882) and brother Paul (1838–1914), followed family tradition when they went to work as young men at the Royal Armory in the Kingdom of Wurttemberg, part of pre-unification Germany. Paul proved the more accomplished of the pair and in the 1890s developed bolt-action rifles known for reliability and ease of use. Mauser rifles fired metallic cartridges, a significant improvement over the accident-prone paper cartridges used in earlier weapons such as the Dreyse needle gun.

Paul Mauser initially made single-shot weapons that were deemed inferior to repeaters sold by Winchester and others. This inspired him to come out with magazine-fed variations. The best of the repeat-fire Mausers, the Gewehr Model 1898, allowed for even faster shooting because it featured a disposable stripper clip preloaded with five smokeless cartridges. The German army adopted the Gewehr 98 during World War I. Mauser also made pistols, including the 7.63mm C96, which had a distinctive appearance: a box magazine in front of the trigger and a grip that resembled a broom handle. The C96 came with a removable shoulder stock that doubled as a carrying case. Among its famous users was Winston Churchill, who carried the weapon in the Sudan and the Second Boer War. Of his Mauser, Churchill said: "The pistol was the best thing in the world."

Wilhelm (left) and Paul Mauser combined their unique talents to produce the Mauser line of weapons.

Tapered barrel

▲ MAUSER KARABINER 1898A BOLT-ACTION RIFLE

Country: Germany

Date: circa 1916

Barrel Length: 23 3/5in

Caliber: .30

The downsized rifle was a better fit for close-combat conditions.

Entire barrel encased in sheet-metal tube

Top-loading, ten-round box magazine

▲ GEWEHR 1888 COMMISSION RIFLE

Country: Germany

Date: 1888–1897

Barrel Length: 29 1/10in

Caliber: .31

▲ MAUSER "BROOMHANDLE" C96

Country: Germany

Date: 1896

Barrel Length: 5 1/2in

Caliber: .30

The C96 semiautomatic offered the highest-velocity commercially–made pistol cartridge until the .357 Magnum was introduced.

Broom-handle grip

Wilhelm and Paul Mauser: Brothers in Arms

▲ **MAUSER MODEL 1914 POCKET PISTOL**

Country:	Germany
Date:	1914
Length:	6in
Caliber:	.30

Single-shot, bolt-action firing mechanism

Detachable shoulder stock converts pistol to carbine

Easily removable telescopic sight

One-piece magazine and frame were costly to make

▲ MAUSER C96 SHOULDER STOCK CARBINE

Country: Germany

Date: 1896

Barrel Length: 5 1/2in

Caliber: .30

The C96 pistol/carbine was used by Winston Churchill in 1898's Battle of Omdurman.

▲ MAUSER GEWEHR SNIPER RIFLE

Country: Germany

Date: circa 1916

Barrel Length: 29 1/10in

Caliber: .30

Fitted with advanced telescopic sights, this bolt-action Mauser was used by German snipers.

Fitted with a pistol grip and forward bipod to manage the long barrel

▲ MAUSER ANTI-TANK RIFLE

Country: Germany

Date: 1917

Barrel Length: 38 3/4in

Caliber: .50

This .50-caliber armor-piercing rifle was Germany's response to the newly introduced British tank.

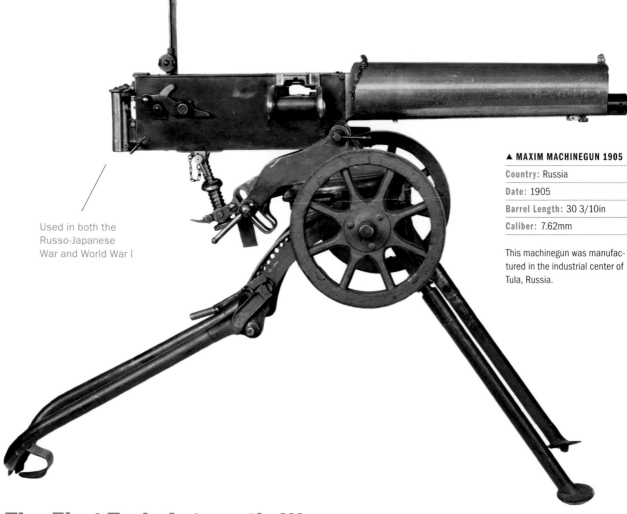

Used in both the
Russo-Japanese
War and World War I

▲ **MAXIM MACHINEGUN 1905**

Country: Russia

Date: 1905

Barrel Length: 30 3/10in

Caliber: 7.62mm

This machinegun was manufactured in the industrial center of
Tula, Russia.

The First Truly Automatic Weapon

HARNESSING THE RECOIL ENERGY OF FIRED BULLETS, AN INVENTOR REALIZED THE CENTURIES-
OLD AMBITION TO PRODUCE A GUN THAT COULD OPERATE CONTINUOUSLY, AND LETHALLY.

The first manually operated, multibarrel, rapid-fire gun to see action in the United States was the Gatling Gun, invented during the Civil War by physician Richard Gatling. But credit for the first truly automatic weapons that merited the label "machinegun" belongs to inventor and engineer Hiram Maxim, an American who moved to the United Kingdom in midlife.

It was while he was living in England that Maxim figured out how to harness the energy of a fired bullet. The explosive force that propels a round out of the barrel also drives the gun itself backward. Rather than viewing this recoil energy as a detriment—the traditional opinion of gun designers and shooters—Maxim put the extra energy to use, assembling a mechanism that

automatically ejected the spent casing and then loaded a fresh cartridge. As long as the shooter kept the trigger depressed, this cycle repeated itself.

Introduced in 1884, the original Maxim Gun required a crew of several operators who fired bullets from a continuous ammunition belt. At up to 600 rounds a minute, the furious rate of fire generated enough heat to damage or even melt steel, so

In 1888 the Prince of Wales fired Hiram Maxim's 1884 machinegun, with the inventor by his side. Thirteen years later, the prince, then King Edward VII, knighted Maxim.

◄ CHAUCHAT LIGHT MACHINEGUN

Country: France

Date: circa 1915

Barrel Length: 18 1/2in

Caliber: .30

The Chauchat, which pioneered the pistol grip and detachable magazine, was plagued by design flaws.

Wooden rifle-style shoulder stock

Fired up to 600 rounds per minute

Maxim devised a water-filled jacket to surround and cool the barrel. The Maxim Gun typically was perched on a collapsible two- or three-legged stand, and was more manageable than the bulky, multibarrel Gatling, which resembled an artillery piece and required a wheeled chassis to transport. In 1904 and 1905, Russian forces deployed the .45-caliber Maxim

Gun in the Russo-Japanese War, foreshadowing the devastating effect of machineguns in World War I.

The U.S. Army began issuing four machineguns to each of its regiments in 1912. By the end of World War I, that allotment had grown to more than 300 machineguns per regiment. Many of the great names in Western firearm development applied their

genius to refining and manufacturing automatic weapons. In April 1917, when the United States entered the Great War, military authorities in Washington commissioned a company called Marlin Arms to make a machinegun invented by American designer John Browning. That weapon, known as the Colt-Browning Model 1895, relied on a gas-driven

A soldier tested a Lewis machinegun on a Marine Corps rifle range in 1917.

Hiram Maxim: An Inventive Spirit

As a young man, Hiram Maxim (1840–1916) was knocked over by a rifle's recoil, an incident which according to legend inspired his most famous invention: the machinegun.

Like many other firearm pioneers, Maxim was a free-ranging spirit. In addition to the Maxim Gun, he patented the gun silencer, hair-curling irons, a mousetrap, and a popular fairground ride called the Captive Flying Machine.

Some advised him to narrow his focus. "In 1882 when I was in Vienna," Maxim is reported to have said, "I met an American whom I had known in the States. He said: 'Hang your chemistry and electricity! If you want to make a pile of money, invent something that will enable these Europeans to cut each other's throats with greater facility.'"

Before World War I, European forces proved the brutal efficiency of Maxim's weapon in colonial warfare. In the Matabele War of 1893–1894, in what is today Zimbabwe, it was reported that 50 British troops with four Maxims fought off 5,000 Ndebele warriors. In the Battle of Omdurman in 1898 in Sudan, another small British force reportedly killed more than 10,000 Arabs. That year, the Anglo-French writer Hilaire Belloc penned the poem "The Modern Traveller," capturing the European spirit: "Whatever happens, we have got/ The Maxim gun, and they have not."

▲ LEWIS MARK 1 MACHINEGUN

Country: Belgium, Great Britain, United States

Date: circa 1914–1942

Barrel Length: 26 2/5in

Caliber: .30

The gun's distinctive "taka-taka-taka" sound earned it the nickname "the Belgian rattlesnake." It weighed 26 pounds and could be carried by one soldier.

piston that moved back and forth beneath the barrel. As a result, it had to sit fairly high off the ground on top of a tripod, an arrangement that made its several-man crew vulnerable to the enemy. Without the tripod, the piston would scrape the ground, causing some troops to dub the Colt-Browning the "potato-digger."

The British army of World War I adopted the Colt Vickers machinegun, a .303-caliber, water-cooled model based on the Maxim design. At 83 pounds, it required a team of six soldiers to lug it around, set up its tripod, and fire. The British also acquired a more portable weapon called the Lewis Light Machine Gun, designed by Noah Lewis of the U.S. Army in 1911. The .303-caliber Lewis had a tubular 50-round magazine mounted on top of the barrel. Allied forces equipped some airplanes with Lewis guns, and U.S. ground forces used a .30-caliber version.

The German Spandau Maxim, named for the Imperial German arsenal at Spandau, fired 7.92mm belt-fed rounds via a water-cooled barrel. Germans mounted the guns on their airplanes and synchronized the firing mechanism so that it could shoot through the spinning propeller. Not all machineguns were effective, of course. The French Chauchat, which had a distinctive crescent-shaped magazine, proved to be both inaccurate and prone to malfunction. When American troops were given some of the weapons, they derided them as "sho-shos," a phonetic play on Chauchat, and tossed them aside.

Combined with heavy-volume artillery shelling, machinegun fire made the battlefields of Europe a deafening, bloody hell. Machineguns encouraged both sides to dig deep trenches that led to lengthy stalemates. Maxim's creations and their descendants were ideal for relatively small machinegun crews (protected by a detachment of armed infantrymen) to defend a dug-in or elevated position and efficiently mow down foes. In this manner, machineguns industrialized killing and helped strip modern warfare of whatever romance might still attach to the institution. Along with such innovations as poison gas and incessant shelling, the machinegun inflicted psychological as well as physical wounds.

▼ LEWIS LIGHT MACHINEGUN

Country:	United States
Date:	circa 1916
Barrel Length:	34 1/4 in
Caliber:	.30

This Lewis was made by the U.S.-based Savage Arms and shipped to Russia around 1916.

Nicknamed "the potato digger" because it burrowed into the ground if improperly positioned

Air instead of water was used to cool the rapid-fire gun.

▼ VICKERS MK1 MACHINEGUN

Country: Great Britain

Date: 1912

Barrel Length: 28in

Caliber: .303

Crews of six men were needed to move the Vickers and its water-cooling system and tripod.

Ammunition belt feeder

◄ COLT BROWNING M1895 MACHINEGUN

Country: United States

Date: 1895

Barrel Length: 28in

Caliber: .30

The M1895 saw action under Teddy Roosevelt in the Spanish-American War but was considered obsolete in the United States by World War, I when it was used only for training new recruits and for export.

▲ COLT MODEL 1911

Country: United States	
Date: 1911	
Barrel Length: 5in	
Caliber: .45	

The M1911 and its variant, the M1911A1, remained the main U.S. service arm into the 1980s.

Semiautomatic Handguns and Revolvers

FIREARMS DESIGNERS FOLLOWED THE LEAD OF HIRAM MAXIM IN DEVELOPING SELF-LOADING PISTOLS THAT RELIED ON RECOIL ENERGY.

While most infantry fighters carried bolt-action rifles, officers, logistical-support troops, and tank crews armed themselves with handguns. Even when they weren't standard-issue for front-line soldiers in the trenches, many infantrymen tried to obtain handguns for use in close combat. Machinegun crews also sometimes carried handguns to defend themselves in case their

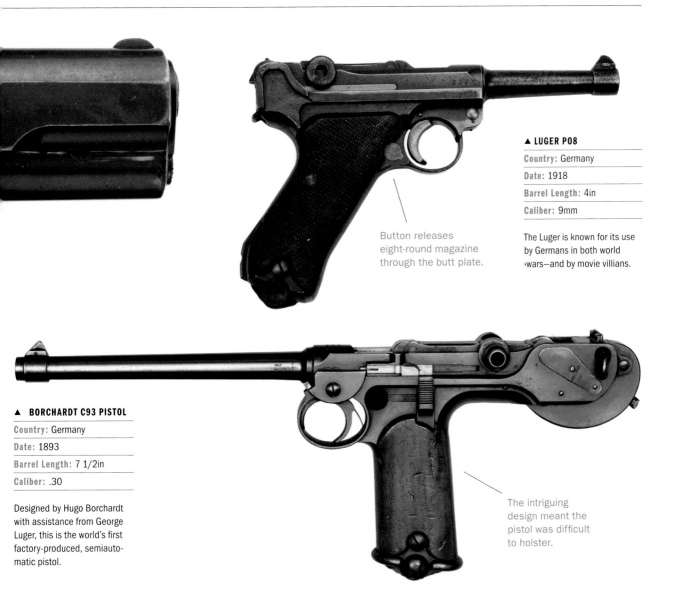

▲ **LUGER P08**

Country: Germany

Date: 1918

Barrel Length: 4in

Caliber: 9mm

The Luger is known for its use by Germans in both world wars—and by movie villians.

Button releases eight-round magazine through the butt plate.

▲ **BORCHARDT C93 PISTOL**

Country: Germany

Date: 1893

Barrel Length: 7 1/2in

Caliber: .30

Designed by Hugo Borchardt with assistance from George Luger, this is the world's first factory-produced, semiauto-matic pistol.

The intriguing design meant the pistol was difficult to holster.

positions were overrun.

The British remained devoted to revolvers that resembled the 19th-century creations of Colt and Smith & Wesson. The Birmingham manufacturer Webley & Scott made a .455-caliber double-action revolver with a six-round cylinder that U.K. officers carried in the Second Boer War and again in World War I. Some German officers were armed with

similar .44-caliber, six-shot revolvers.

In contrast, the self-loading pistol represented a notable jump forward in handgun technology, benefiting from the insights Hiram Maxim applied to the machinegun. A variety of firearm designers in Europe and the United States scaled down the Maxim idea of using recoil energy to load, fire, eject, and reload a weapon's cartridge. Unlike fully

automatic machineguns, though, self-loading pistols are more accurately described as "semiautomatic." That's because these handguns do not fire a continuous stream of bullets. Instead, each pull of the trigger results in a single shot.

Hugo Borchardt, an American designer of German descent, used the Maxim recoil principle for a pistol introduced in 1893 that fired 7.65mm

Checkered grip

▲ CASTELLI REVOLVER

Country: Italy

Date: 1889

Barrel Length: 4 1/2in

Caliber: .41

This compact Italian service revolver incorporated a folding trigger. Here, the trigger is in the folded position.

Octagonal barrel

OPEN VIEW

▶ P. WEBLEY & SON PRYSE REVOLVER

Country: Great Britain

Date: circa 1877

Caliber: .45

This gun is a rare collector's item.

cartridges from a magazine housed in its grip. Georg Luger, an employee of Deutsch Waffen & Munitions Fabriken in Germany, improved on the Borchardt model with a pistol that would famously bear his name and was first adopted by the Swiss military in 1900 for use with a 7.65mm round. When the German army adopted the Luger-designed

P08 model in 1908, it preferred larger, more powerful ammunition: the 9mm "parabellum," a term taken from a Latin phrase *Si vis pacem, parabellum*, which translates as "If you want peace, prepare for war." Used by German officers in both world wars, Lugers became a favorite take-home trophy of American troops and an emblem of Nazi evil.

John Browning, an American gun designer, addressed the need for more powerful cartridges when he turned his attention to semiautomatic pistols in the early 1900s. Manufactured by Colt, Browning's .45-caliber became known as the M1911 when the U.S. Army adopted it that year. The Colt .45 acquired legendary status equivalent to that of earlier Colt and

Bone-handled grip

OPEN VIEW

▲ MONTENEGRIN REVOLVER

Country: Austria

Date: 1914

Barrel Length: 5in

Caliber: .44

Fearing invasion by more powerful neighbors, King Nicholas of Montenegro ordered male citizens to obtain this revolver.

▲ WEBLEY MARK VI

Country: Great Britain

Date: 1915

Barrel length: 6in

Caliber: .45

This was the standard British service revolver through World War I and World War II.

Lugers became favorite take-home trophies of American troops and an emblem of Nazi evil.

Smith & Wesson revolvers. Many American soldiers carried the M1911 pistol during World War I. With slight adjustments and improvements—such as an arch in the mainspring housing to force the web of the hand higher into the safety grip—the M1911 remained standard-issue in World War II, the Korean War, and the Vietnam War—an extraordinary example of firearm longevity. The gun's cartridge, also designed by Browning and known as the ACP (Automatic Colt Pistol), propelled a bullet with twice the force of the 9mm rounds favored in Europe. The M1911 carried seven rounds in its spring-loaded magazine in the grip; the shooter could load an eighth round in the chamber.

John Moses Browning: Starting Young

Few men had a greater influence on 20th-century firearms than John Moses Browning (1855–1926). During an amazingly prolific career, Browning helped shape practically every category of small arms, selling his firearm designs to manufacturers ranging from Colt to Winchester to Fabrique Nationale of Belgium.

The son of a pioneer Mormon family, Browning made his first gun as a 13-year-old in his father's shop in Ogden, Utah. Eleven years later, in 1879, he was awarded the first of his 128 gun patents. In the 1880s, Browning designed single-shot and repeating rifles for Winchester, as well as the first effective repeating shotgun. In the late 1880s, he turned his attention to automatic weapons and designed a machinegun that used the high-pressure gas generated by the firing of the cartridge to extract and eject the spent round, replacing it with a fresh one. He sold that design to Colt and it became the Colt M1895 machinegun, capable of firing 400 rounds a minute through an air-cooled barrel. Among his other creations were the Model 1917 recoil-operated, water-cooled machinegun; the Browning Automatic Rifle, or BAR, a light machinegun introduced in 1918; the M1911 semiautomatic pistol used by the U.S. military during World War I and for decades thereafter; the Browning .50-caliber machinegun; and the Browning Auto-5, a semiautomatic shotgun. With only modest modifications, versions of these firearms are still manufactured today by a wide variety of companies.

Browning died of a heart attack on November 26, 1926, while at his workbench tinkering with a new self-loading pistol for Fabrique Nationale in Liege, Belgium. Even that 9mm weapon turned out to be a posthumous success when it was completed in 1935 and marketed as the FN Browning HP 35, also known as the Browning Hi-Power.

John Browning, with his M1917 machinegun. He is credited with obtaining 128 patents and creating more than 100 weapons during his six-decade career.

It took Browning, second from left, 12 years to convince the U.S. Army to adopt his M1917 machinegun.

Workers polished Browning's Winchester-made guns, circa 1915.

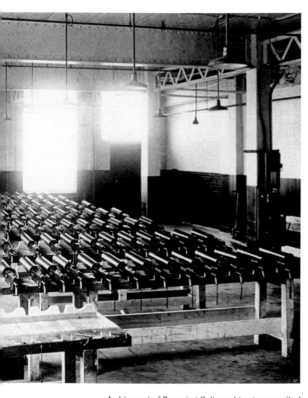
A shipment of Browning-Colt machineguns awaited transport from Bridgeport, Connecticut, in 1918. The weapons were used by Belgians and Russians throughout World War I.

Browning's workbench in his Utah gunsmith shop, circa 1900.

Browning's Colt M1911, here with its magazine, is unmatched in longevity.

A Canadian machinegun crew with a Colt-Browning.

Trench Warfare

USED FOR SHELTER AND TO DELIVER SUPPLIES, THE NETWORKS
ALSO HOUSED MACHINEGUN EMPLACEMENTS.

Between machinegun fire and rapid-firing artillery pieces, the quantity of ordnance on the Western Front was so overwhelming that trenches were necessary for survival. Food, ammunition, fresh troops and mail arrived via trench, which also housed command posts. The first major trench lines were completed in late November 1914, and at their peak, trenches used by both sides extended almost 400 miles from the Belgian coast to Switzerland.

German troops hunkered down in France in 1917.

A British soldier manned his antiaircraft post with trench weapons dangling at his side.

A display of German mortar and trench artillery in France in 1917.

Britain's 15th Brigade in northern France in July 1918.

German infantry passed through captured French territory, March 1918.

A French soldier on guard in 1916.

A Scottish officer leads his men toward battle in France in 1917.

Hollywood Firearms

GUNS INVENTED AROUND THE TURN OF THE CENTURY AND USED
DURING WORLD WAR I MADE THEIR WAY INTO POPULAR CULTURE.

Charlie Chaplin with a Krag-Jørgensen in Shoulder Arms.

The weapons of the Great War, like the Mauser C96, Luger P08, and Browning M1911, have lent credibility to a wide variety of films, starting with 1935's *G Men*, in which James Cagney as Brick Davis wields a Browning M1911. Other actors also carried the M1911, including Humphrey Bogart as Rick Blaine in *Casablanca* (1942) and Leonardo DiCaprio as Jay Gatsby in *The Great Gatsby* (2013).

Another gun with a film role is the SMLE. That is the weapon Henry Fonda, playing the hesitant Canadian Corporal Colin Spence, carries in *Immortal Sergeant* (1943), set in the North African campaign of World War II. And then there's the Mauser C96: You can see a youthful Lieutenant Winston Churchill, played by Simon Ward, carrying the distinctive "broomhandle" auto-loading pistol in *Young Winston* (1972).

Three weeks after World War II ended, John Wayne debuted in Back to Bataan with a Colt M1921 tommy gun.

Simon Ward in 1972's Young Winston *with a Mauser C96. semi-*

Henry Fonda with his SMLE rifle in 1943's Immortal Sergeant.

Thomas Mitchell (center) posed with a Vickers machinegun for the 1943 film Bataan. *To his right is Robert Taylor. Surrounding them, clockwise from left, are M1917-toting Phillip Terry, Lloyd Nolan, Lee Bowman, Robert Walker, and Desi Arnaz with a Springfield rifle.*

Organized-crime fighter Eliot Ness formed a team known as the Untouchables to target Al Capone and his gang.

Between the Wars

GANGLAND VIOLENCE, BANK ROBBERIES, AND AN ASSASSINATION ATTEMPT ON
PRESIDENT FRANKLIN ROOSEVELT LED TO EARLY GUN-CONTROL LEGISLATION.

The end of World War I ushered in an era of peace around the globe, but at home in the United States, Prohibition sparked a wave of violence in the streets as gangsters and federal agents battled it out over illicit booze—often, but not only, with guns.

Two figures, Al Capone (1899–1947) and Eliot Ness (1903–1957), personified the two extremes of the period. Capone, the notorious Chicago crime boss, was a street-smart thug who ran many of the city's most lucrative illegal breweries and stills. Ness was an ambitious University of Chicago grad who followed his brother-in-law into federal law enforcement. He joined the Treasury Department's Bureau of Prohibition with a mission: to stop Capone at any cost.

Aided by wiretaps and informants, Ness's elite squad of Treasury agents, nicknamed "the Untouchables" for their reputation for resisting bribes, aggressively raided Capone's operations. In retaliation, Ness was targeted several times for assassination, and one of his best friends was killed.

An Era's Well Known Weapons

The antagonists in the Chicago Prohibition wars relied on a common selection of firearms. The swift-firing Thompson 1928 submachinegun became the most notorious weapon of the time, responsible for countless

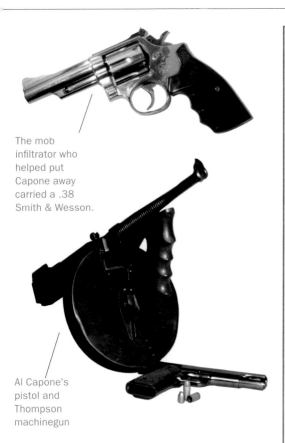

The mob infiltrator who helped put Capone away carried a .38 Smith & Wesson.

Al Capone's pistol and Thompson machinegun

Christian temperance supporters in Pasadena, California, fought liquor with prayer.

In White Plains, New York, a public "alcohol banning" booth

deaths, including some fatalties during the Saint Valentine's Day Massacre of 1929 among rival gang members from Chicago's North Side. The tommy gun, named for its inventor, John Thompson, featured a 50-round drum magazine containing potent .45-caliber ACP cartridges. Double-barreled shotguns were also popular on both sides of the law, and gangsters favored sawed-off versions that were concealable beneath long coats.

Another weapon adapted from the military to urban law enforcement (and organized crime) was the Colt semiautomatic 1911, which had a seven-round magazine and also fired powerful .45-caliber rounds. It first saw action as a sidearm in World War I. An improved model, the 1911A1, was issued to soldiers in World War II.

Prohibition and Crime

The 18th Amendment and the dubious policy of banning alcohol in the United States from 1920 to 1933 reflected the reform impulses of social progressives and the organizational skills of such activist groups as the Anti-Saloon League and the Women's Christian Temperance Union.

But while the general public was unenthusiastic about the ban, organized crime was much cheered by the new "dry" laws. Previously focused on prostitution, gambling, protection rackets, and ordinary theft, gangs led by Italian and Irish immigrants swiftly assembled bootlegging operations in the 1920s to feed the thirst of the non–law abiding citizenry. Rather than reforming morals, Prohibition heightened crime levels and glamorized the outlaws who profited from failed abstention.

Among the gangsters who dined out on Prohibition were Al Capone, Lucky Luciano, Meyer Lansky and his partner Bugsy Siegel, Arnold Rothstein, and Enoch "Nucky" Johnson of Atlantic City.

Smith & Wesson made inroads in the expanding marketplace for police weapons with the S&W Registered Magnum, a .357-caliber revolver both powerful and precise. The six-round Registered Magnum, later known as the Model 27, weighed less than two pounds and was accurate to 150 feet. Unsurprisingly, it soon became popular with the bad guys as well as G-men and local cops.

It's worth noting that Mob enforcers did not restrict themselves to firearms. If broken bones were called for, a thick-barreled Louisville Slugger baseball bat would do the trick. To show that a protection racket meant business—*it sure would be a shame if that nice candy store were to burn down*—a crudely fashioned Molotov cocktail (a glass bottle filled with gasoline, topped by a piece of cloth that doubled as a stopper and wick) did all the damage that was necessary.

In the end, though, it wasn't firepower or any kind of brute force that brought Capone to heel. Ness's Untouchables kept Capone busy and put a dent in his illegal liquor business, but careful research by the Internal Revenue Service produced the tax-evasion charges that finally sent the gangster to prison in 1932. His incarceration did little to stem the street violence that plagued Chicago and other major American cities.

The National Firearms Act

In 1934, the year after Prohibition ended, President Franklin Delano Roosevelt signed into law the National Firearms Act, a response to the shocking gangland violence, bank robberies, and an assassination

Clockwise from left: Al Capone's weapons were seized by Joliet, Illinois, police in 1927; Capone's fellow mobster, "West Side" Frankie Pope, was carried in a stretcher; Bugs Moran, a Capone rival whose associates were gunned down February 14, 1929, in the Saint Valentine's Day Massacre; The Chicago Daily News covered the killings; victims of the hit.

Bonnie Parker and Clyde Barrow: Armed and Dangerous

The outlaws Bonnie Parker (1910–1934) and Clyde Barrow (1909–1934) lived violent lives robbing banks, stores, and gas stations. Yet Bonnie and Clyde, as they were known, became glamorous antiheroes of the Great Depression—symbols of antiestablishment defiance even as they victimized struggling business owners and ordinary lawmen.

Much about their myth, however, had little connection to reality. Bonnie Parker, for example, was reputed to smoke cigars and wield a machinegun. She did neither.

Bonnie and Clyde and their accomplices were merciless killers, though. Barrow favored a military-issued Browning Automatic Rifle stolen from a National Guard armory in Oklahoma and used the BAR in several shoot-outs with lawmen.

The couple finally was stopped in May 1934 by a back-road ambush in a Louisiana parish, arranged by officers of that state and Texas. One of the posse members described the carnage: "Each of us six officers had a shotgun and an automatic rifle and pistols. We opened fire with the automatic rifles. They were emptied before (Barrow's) car got even with us. Then we used shotguns… After shooting the shotguns, we emptied the pistols at the car… We weren't taking any chances."

attempt on FDR in 1933. The act strictly regulated the civilian sale and possession of weapons associated with Capone and his ilk: machineguns, concealable short-barreled rifles and sawed-off shotguns, and sound suppressors.

Conventional pistols and revolvers, as well as full-length shotguns and rifles, were not covered by the NFA, however, and that limited the act's effectiveness. Even after passage of the NFA, the debate over gun control in the United States did not heat up immediately. Civilian gun ownership remained common in rural areas and among veterans of military service. Many high schools sponsored rifle teams, without a hint of controversy. Rising urban crime in the 1960s, combined with social unrest and the assassinations of President John F. Kennedy; his brother Robert, a former attorney general; and the civil rights champion Martin Luther King rekindled calls for stricter regulation of civilian-owned firearms. That debate continues to the present day.

WORLD WAR II, A GREAT GENERATION OF GUNS

THE NAZIS INTRODUCED THE ASSAULT RIFLE, BUT THE QUALITY AND QUANTITY
OF AMERICAN WEAPONS GAVE THE ALLIES A CRITICAL ADVANTAGE.

Marines bombing a Japanese outpost in the 1945 battle for Iwo Jima. The 36-day fight led to 27,000 American and 18,000 Japanese casualties. In the quiet of the aftermath, an American officer observed: "Hell with the fire out, but still smoking."

Overpowering Hitler

WEAPON DESIGNERS MADE GREAT ADVANCES WITH
MACHINEGUNS AND VERSATILE RIFLES.

World War II hastened the pace of weapons innovation, firearms included, with predictably devastating effect. From 1939 through 1945, warring armies suffered 25 million casualties. Thirty million civilians died as a direct result of fighting and bombing, while disease and starvation caused another 20 million civilian fatalities. In absolute terms, World War II is the most lethal conflict humankind has ever seen.

At the more scientifically advanced end of the weapons spectrum, the U.S. development and use of the atomic bomb to force Japan's surrender in 1945 changed forever the calculus of war and geopolitics. In a far more modest development, the U.S. Army replaced the bolt-action rifle with a self-loading (semiautomatic) model as the standard infantry weapon. The reliable M1 Garand allowed American GIs to achieve higher rates of fire while maintaining accuracy at a distance.

The Germans didn't lack for inventiveness, gaining an edge in machinegun proficiency with the feared MG42. Germany also developed the versatile Sturmgewehr ("storm" or "assault" rifle) 44, which combined the attributes of a submachinegun's rapid fire with the handiness of an infantry weapon.

In the end, American industrial might overwhelmed that of Germany and the other Axis powers. The quality and sheer quantity of American weaponry outmatched what Hitler's factories could produce. This capacity allowed the United States to sustain Great Britain during its darkest hours in 1940 and 1941 and, after the U.S. committed its own forces, to compel Germany and Japan to submit.

A U.S. flotilla converged on Normandy's Omaha Beach after D-Day fighting forced the Germans to retreat.

Americans surged onto a Normandy beach a few days after the June 6, 1944, offensive.

U.S. Marine Raiders helped drive the Japanese off the Solomon Islands in 1943.

U.S. Army soldiers manned antiaircraft artillery in North Africa in 1943.

THE WORLD AT WAR

Approximately 690 million people from around the globe served during World War II, including 16 million Americans.

1936 October: Nazi Germany and fascist Italy signed a treaty that became the basis of the Axis powers.

1938 September: Germany incorporated Austria; Britain and France signed the Munich Agreement, ceding portions of Czechoslovakia to Germany

1940 July: Germany attacked France, leading to an armistice, with Nazis occupying the northern half of the country and the collaborationist Vichy regime governing the south.

| 1935 | 1936 | 1937 | 1938 | 1939 | 1940 |

1937 July: Japan invaded China, starting the war in the Pacific.

1939 September: Germany invaded Poland, formally starting World War II in Europe, as Britain and France declared war on Germany; the Soviets invaded Poland from the east.

1943 July: U.S. and British troops landed in Sicily; Soviets liberated Kiev.

1944 (clockwise from upper left) June: Allied troops liberated Rome; August: U.S. troops marched down the Champs-Élysées; December: Germans launched the Battle of the Bulge, a final and ultimately unsuccessful offensive in the West; August: Allied troops in Paris.

1942 November: A Soviet counterattack near Stalingrad trapped Nazis and began to turn the tide.

| 1941 | 1942 | 1943 | 1944 | 1945 | 1946 |

1941 December: Germany invaded the Soviet Union; Japan bombed Pearl Harbor; the United States declared war on Japan. Germany and its Axis partners declared war on America.

1945 May: Soviets captured Warsaw; Soviets encircled Berlin; Hitler committed suicide.

1945 May: Germany surrendered to the Allies.

1945 August: The U.S. dropped an atomic bomb on Hiroshima and three days later another one on Nagasaki; Japan agreed in principle to unconditional surrender.

1945 September: Japan formally surrendered, ending World War II.

Internal magazine held
an eight-round clip

Germany's standard
infantry rifle

Fitted for
a bayonet
or grenade
launcher

Dawn of the Battle Rifle

EACH COUNTRY'S GUNS WERE UNIQUE, BUT EVEN THE UPGRADED MAUSER
AND ARISAKA WERE ECLIPSED BY THE AMERICANS' SUPERIOR M1 GARAND.

Most militaries entered World War II equipping their troops with World War I–era manually operated repeating rifles. Americans received the Springfield 1903 bolt-action; British, a shortened version of the Lee-Enfield Mark 1; Germans, a member of the Mauser family; and Japanese, a weapon in vogue during the turn-of-the-century Russo-Japanese War. Over the course of the war, militaries moved toward more advanced self-loading, or semiautomatic, rifles like the American M1 Garand, equipped with an eight-round clip of .30-caliber cartridges.

Germany

The German *wehrmacht*, or infantry, initially armed its soldiers with upgraded versions of Mauser bolt-action rifles such as the Karabiner 98K, which fired a standard 7.92mm Mauser round. More than 14 million were manufactured between 1935 and 1945, with variations for paratroopers and snipers. In 1948, the Mauser factory

▲ M1 GARAND

Country: United States

Date: 1945

Barrel Length: 24in

Caliber: .30

Garand semiautomatics easily outfired the slower bolt-action rifles of the Germans, Japanese, and Italians.

▼ MAUSER KARABINER 98K

Country: Germany

Date: 1942

Barrel Length: 23.5in

Caliber: 7.92mm

Soviets captured millions of Mauser 98Ks by war's end.

Effective range up to 500 yards

▼ ENFIELD NO. 4 MARK 1

Country: Great Britain

Date: 1939

Barrel Length: 25 1/5in

Caliber: .30

Britain's modified infantry rifle was also manufactured in the United States and Canada.

was dismantled, although some of the machinery was salvaged and used by the German manufacturer today known as Heckler & Koch. In 1943, the German army introduced the Gewehr 43, a 7.92 x 57mm self-loading rifle that increased firepower with its 10-round detachable box magazine.

Japan

The Japanese relied on a bolt-action model dating to 1905 and called the Arisaka Type 38/44, because it was introduced in the 38th year of the Emperor Meiji's reign (a naming convention unique to the Japanese) and updated in 1944. A derivative of the Mauser, the Arisaka fired a

6.5mm round. It was replaced later by a more powerful 7.7mm version known as the Type 99. The 99 had an unusual folding monopod attached to the front of the wooden stock. The Japanese military experimented with copies of the U.S. M1 Garand semiautomatic—referred to as the Type 4 and Type 5—but did not

▼ WALTHER GEWEHR 43

Country: Germany

Date: 1943

Barrel Length: 22in

Caliber: 7.92mm

The G43, with its optical sight, was issued primarily to snipers.

▶ ARISAKA TYPE 38

Country: Japan

Date: 1905

Barrel Length: 31 1/2in

Caliber: .25

perfect their versions in time for widespread use in World War II.

United States

American GIs carried a superior .30-caliber semiautomatic rifle named for its inventor, John Garand. The M1 Garand fired one bullet for each pull of the trigger, but with its eight-round disposable en bloc (a French term meaning self-contained) clip, a soldier could reload rapidly and fire up to 40 bullets a minute.

After the eighth round, the en bloc clip would automatically eject upward, making a distinctive "ping!" sound. By the end of the war, U.S. factories had produced more than five million M1s. In 1942, the U.S. Army introduced a lighter M1 carbine for use by officers, tank crews, and truck drivers. With an 18-inch barrel, this intermediate-size weapon was more manageable than a 24-inch-barrel infantry rifle while still being able to fire a cartridge

with more range than M1911 pistol ammunition.

Great Britain

The British, meanwhile, armed their infantrymen with updated versions of the Lee-Enfield rifle of World War I vintage. The new Lee-Enfield No. 4, the Mark 1, introduced in 1939, had a modified bolt and receiver and a redesigned rear sight. The exposed muzzle of the No. 4 allowed British designers to customize certain Lee-

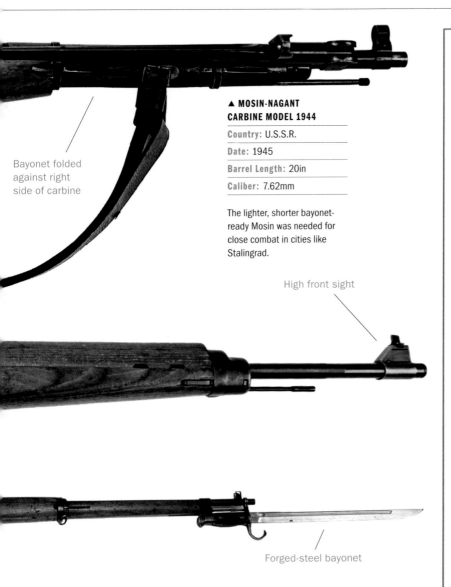

Bayonet folded
against right
side of carbine

▲ **MOSIN-NAGANT
CARBINE MODEL 1944**

Country:	U.S.S.R.
Date:	1945
Barrel Length:	20in
Caliber:	7.62mm

The lighter, shorter bayonet-
ready Mosin was needed for
close combat in cities like
Stalingrad.

High front sight

Forged-steel bayonet

John Garand: Father of the M1

Born in Saint Rémi, Quebec, John Garand (1888–1974) moved with his family to Connecticut as a boy. As a hobby, young Garand enjoyed target shooting and soon applied his knowledge of guns to design work. During World War I, he approached the U.S. War Department, suggesting it manufacture a light machinegun he'd devised. The conflict ended before Garand's invention could get into pro-duction, but his talent landed him a position at the U.S. armory in Spring-field, Massachusetts. There, Garand was asked to focus on a rugged, self-loading infantry rifle. Over more than a dozen years, he perfected a gas-operated prototype patented in 1934, known as the M1 Garand.

In World War II, the M1 gave Ameri-can soldiers an edge in combat as the Garand fired more quickly and accu-rately than standard-issue bolt-action Axis rifles. General George Patton declared the M1 "the greatest battle implement ever devised." The M1 remained the standard U.S. Army rifle through the Korean War and was still being issued during the early 1960s to American troops sent to Vietnam.

Although more than six million M1s were produced, as a government employee, Garand was not entitled to royalties. U.S. lawmakers consid-ered rewarding him with a $100,000 bonus, but the provision never passed Congress.

Enfields to accommodate a tubular antitank grenade launcher. The fin-stabilized grenade could be mounted over the rifle muzzle and fired with a blank cartridge.

Soviet Union

The Russians updated the Mosin-Nagant rifle of 1910 for use in World War II. Designers shortened the barrel to carbine length (20 1/4 inches) and otherwise revamped the weapon to make it less

expensive to manufacture. The final version, the Mosin-Nagant Carbine M1944, had an integral five-round magazine and a folding cruciform bayonet; it fired 7.62 x 54mm rounds. The People's Republic of China continued to knock off the Russian rifle for years after World War II, even after it had become obsolete. The Red Army also issued a self-loading rifle, the 10-round Tokarev SVT40, which was issued to noncommissioned officers and snipers.

Early Assault Rifles

THE STG 44 OFFERED MORE POWER THAN A
SUBMACHINEGUN BUT LESS THAN A BATTLE RIFLE.

The term *sturmgewehr* ("assault rifle") was coined by Adolf Hitler to describe a new type of weapon that addressed the needs of soldiers fighting on urban terrain. Introduced in 1944, the Sturmgewehr 44 (or StG 44) came with a shortened version of the cartridge used in the Mauser M98 battle rifle, had a compact barrel, selective fire (semi- or fully automatic), featured a high capacity detachable magazine and a novel "above barrel" gas system of operation.

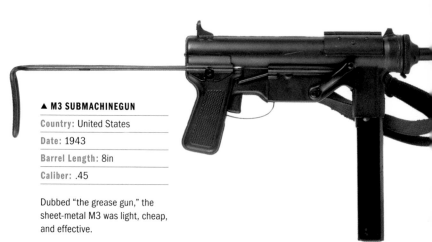

▲ M3 SUBMACHINEGUN

Country: United States

Date: 1943

Barrel Length: 8in

Caliber: .45

Dubbed "the grease gun," the sheet-metal M3 was light, cheap, and effective.

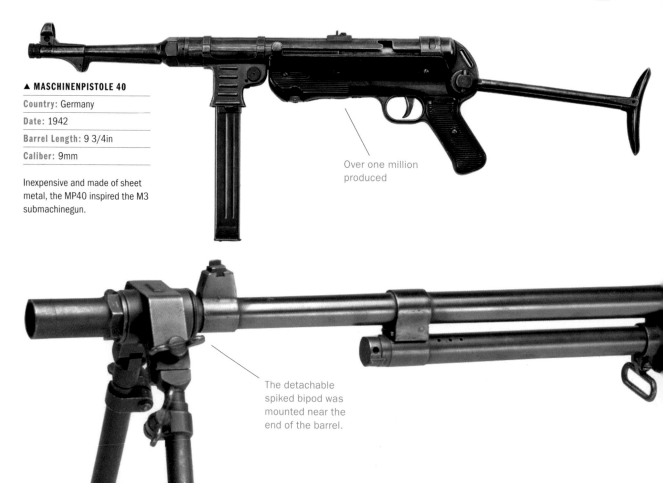

▲ MASCHINENPISTOLE 40

Country: Germany

Date: 1942

Barrel Length: 9 3/4in

Caliber: 9mm

Inexpensive and made of sheet metal, the MP40 inspired the M3 submachinegun.

Over one million produced

The detachable spiked bipod was mounted near the end of the barrel.

Doubled as a
rifle and a light
machinegun

▲ FALLSCHIRMJÄGERGEWEHR 42

Country: Germany

Date: circa 1944

Barrel Length: 19 3/4in

Caliber: 7.92mm

Designed for paratroopers, the
FG42 has an angled grip for aiming
downward.

▼ BROWNING AUTOMATIC
RIFLE M1918A2

Country: United States

Date: 1940

Barrel Length: 24in

Caliber: .30

The BAR, which fired the same
cartridge as the M1 Garand, came
with a 200-page field manual.

▲ STURMGEWEHR 44

Country: Germany

Date: 1945

Barrel Length: 14 3/10

Caliber: 7.92mm

The StG 44 is the predecessor
for modern assault rifles like the
M16 and A-K47.

Carbines and Submachineguns

▶ **SEMIAUTOMATIC M1 CARBINE**

Country: Uniited States

Date: 1941

Barrel Length: 18in

Caliber: .30

Between June 1942 and August 1945, nine primary contractors turned out more than six million versions of this carbine.

One-piece walnut stock

The British destroyed all but a few of these rifles, which were saved for museum display.

Synthetic stock

▲ **SMITH & WESSON LIGHT RIFLE**

Country: United States

Date: 1940

Barrel Length: 9 3/4in

Caliber: .35

The rifles, made for the British, were said to be difficult to operate.

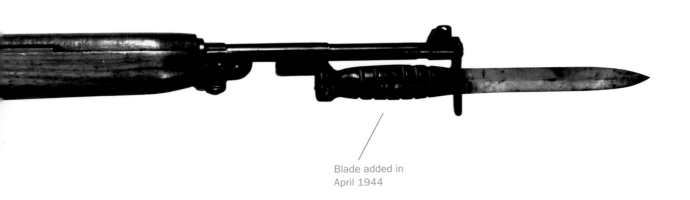

Blade added in
April 1944

One American
officer ordered the
defective Reisings
to be dumped into
Guadalcanal's
rivers.

At the height of the
war, the Soviets
produced 3,000
PPSh-41s a day.

Receiver and barrel
shroud made from
stamped steel

▲ REISING M50
SUBMACHINEGUN

Country: United States

Date: circa 1941

Barrel Length: 14in

Caliber: .45

Easily disabled by dirt and
debris, the Reising was sometimes called 'the poor man's
Thompson."

▼ PPSH-41 SUBMACHINEGUN

Country: Russia

Date: 1941

Barrel Length: 10 3/5in

Caliber: .45

The easily made, user-friendly
PPSh-41 was rushed to Soviet
front-line troops.

▲ THOMPSON M1A1

Country:	United States
Date:	circa 1943
Barrel Length:	10 1/2in
Caliber:	.45

The $200 M1 Thompson (below) was popularized by gangsters in the 1920s, but the simplified, less costly M1A1 (above) was a coveted combat weapon during World War II.

Devising an Improved Machinegun

NEW TECHNOLOGIES ALLOWED USERS TO SHOWER THE ENEMY WITH BULLETS IN A STEADY, DEADLY STREAM.

The product of many minds in many places—including political and military enemies—firearm technology has never advanced in a simple or straight line. Even as John Garand gave U.S. infantry forces an advantage with the self-loading M1, other designers and military leaders turned their attention to refining the crew-manned heavy machinegun and devising a smaller, lighter submachinegun usable by an individual.

The M1 Garand offered long-range accuracy, power, and simplicity. The submachinegun, by contrast, fired less potent pistol-strength cartridges but allowed users to spray bullets steadily and at amazing volumes, achieving greater lethality at close quarters. World War II proved the effectiveness of automatic weapons that could be transported and fired by individual soldiers.

The "Trench Broom"

John T. Thompson, a West Point graduate who worked in the U.S. Army's ordnance department during World War I, advocated development of a handheld automatic weapon. With military bluntness, he referred to his idea as the "trench broom," a lightweight hip- or shoulder-fired machinegun that would "sweep" away the enemy and end the stalemate in Europe.

Army Air Corps trainees practiced firing positions in 1942 with empty Thompsons at Mitchel Field on Long Island, New York, before going to the firing range with real bullets.

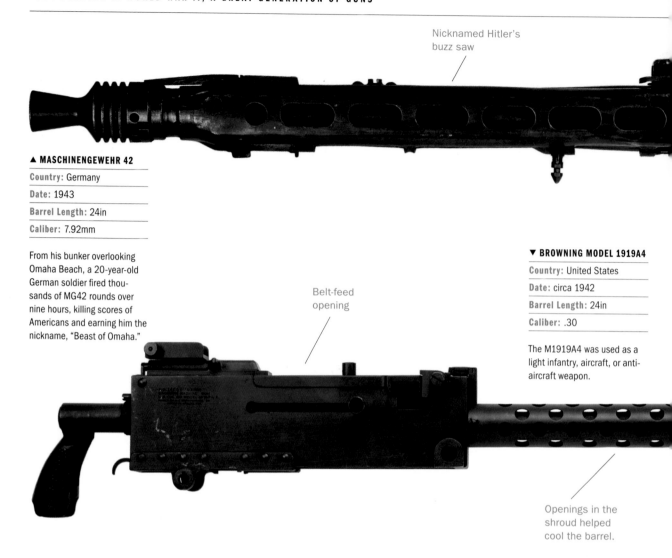

Nicknamed Hitler's buzz saw

▲ MASCHINENGEWEHR 42

Country: Germany

Date: 1943

Barrel Length: 24in

Caliber: 7.92mm

From his bunker overlooking Omaha Beach, a 20-year-old German soldier fired thousands of MG42 rounds over nine hours, killing scores of Americans and earning him the nickname, "Beast of Omaha."

Belt-feed opening

▼ BROWNING MODEL 1919A4

Country: United States

Date: circa 1942

Barrel Length: 24in

Caliber: .30

The M1919A4 was used as a light infantry, aircraft, or anti-aircraft weapon.

Openings in the shroud helped cool the barrel.

The submachinegun Thompson devised fired the same .45-caliber ACP cartridge as the Colt M1911 pistol, but could carry 30 rounds in a stick magazine, which was most common, or 50 rounds in a rotary drum-shaped magazine. Introduced too late for use in World War I, Thompson's creation was adopted in 1928 by the U.S. Navy as the M1928A1. During the interwar years, what Hollywood dubbed the "tommy gun" (a.k.a. the "Chicago typewriter" or just the "chopper") became better known for its appearance in the

hands of Prohibition-era G-men and the gangsters they chased. During the Valentine's Day Massacre of 1929, Al Capone's henchmen used tommy guns to mow down members of a rival syndicate in a Chicago garage. According to tabloid lore, some of the dead were cut nearly in half as a result of the withering hail of bullets.

The Army did eventually adopt an improved version of the tommy gun as the M1A1 submachinegun, which became the standard submachine gun for U.S. troops in World War II, typically with a 20- or

30-round magazine. Less portable than Thompson's submachinegun, the Browning Automatic Rifle, designed by John Browning, packed a more powerful punch. The gas-operated .30-caliber BAR had a 20-round magazine and weighed 20 pounds. Another Browning creation, the M2 automatic, fired .50-caliber rounds with immense stopping power.

Germany's military designers demonstrated an uncanny flair for automatic weapons tailored for individual use. In 1940,

This belt-fed gun could fire between 900 and 1,200 rounds per minute.

▼ BROWNING M2

Country:	United States
Date:	1944
Barrel Length:	36in
Caliber:	.50

After nearly 85 years of service, "Ma Deuce" is still considered one of the world's most effective machineguns.

The M2 was extensively used by U.S. and Allied troops in World War II.

Hitler's armorers introduced the Maschinenpistole 40 (MP40), the first mass-produced standard-issue infantry weapon that didn't have any wooden parts. Confusingly, the highly admired MP40 was colloquially known as the "Schmeisser," although it had not been designed by the famous German designer Hugo Schmeisser. German factories produced some one million MP40s, which were considered superior to such American rivals as the .45-caliber M50 Reising used by some U.S. Marine Corps units.

Named by the Führer
Introduced in 1943, the German Sturmgewehr, or assault rifle, represented the most advanced automatic weapon of its era for an individual soldier. Heavily used against the Soviets on the Eastern Front, the "selective fire" weapon could issue a stream of bullets in fully automatic mode or one round per trigger pull in semiauto mode. It fired a 7.92mm cartridge from a 30-round magazine. (The crew-served, belt-fed MG42 machinegun generally was fired

from a bipod or tripod and could fire up to 1,200 rounds a minute.) Hitler himself bestowed the Sturmgewehr title on the MP44, thinking that the forbidding name would have propaganda value. In the decades after World War II, the Sturmgewehr became the basis for more modern assault rifles such as the Soviet AK-47 and the American M16. But luckily for the Allies, Hitler's favorite arrived on the battlefield too late to turn the tide for the deteriorating Axis powers in 1944 and 1945.

Audie Murphy's Triumph

AN INFANTRY COMMANDER SINGLE-HANDEDLY HELD OFF
AN ENTIRE COMPANY OF NAZIS WITH HIS M1 CARBINE.

World War II hero Audie Murphy (1925–1971) received every military combat award handed out by the U.S. Army, as well as medals from the French and Belgian governments. The product of a poor family in Texas, Murphy aspired to soldiering from boyhood. His first attempts to enlist after the Japanese attack on Pearl Harbor in December 1941 failed, as all three branches of the military—Army, Navy, and Marine Corps—turned him down as underage and underweight. In June 1942, he finally won acceptance into the Army. After several years of distinguished and much-honored service in the Mediterranean and European theaters, Murphy had his greatest moment of glory in January 1945 at the age of 19 when he single-handedly held off an entire company of German soldiers for about an hour during a battle at what was known as the Colmar Pocket in France.

As a 3rd Infantry Division company commander, Murphy ordered his men to retreat to covered positions in the woods while he remained alone at his forward post, firing an M1 carbine and using his field telephone to direct Allied artillery fire. Murphy then mounted an abandoned, burning M-10 tank destroyer and began firing its .50-caliber machinegun at the advancing enemy. Reportedly, he killed or wounded 50 German soldiers and retreated only after he'd been wounded in the leg and ran out of ammunition. Disregarding his injury, he rejoined his men and led them in a successful counteroffensive

Audie Murphy, celebrated for his battlefield heroics in France, replayed some of those World War II scenes in 1955's To Hell and Back.

against the German unit.

For these actions, he received the U.S. Medal of Honor and was promoted to first lieutenant. After the war, Murphy went on to a successful career as an actor, playing himself in *To Hell and Back* (1955), but also suffered from what today would probably be diagnosed as post-traumatic stress disorder. He slept with a loaded pistol, was addicted to sleeping pills, and late in life had money trouble. He died in a plane crash before his 46th birthday.

Winston Churchill Aims to Raise Morale

He looked like a Chicago gangster of the 1920s: pinstripe suit, fat cigar, and tommy gun. The iconic image of Prime Minister Winston Churchill of Great Britain holding a Thompson submachinegun was not, however, a nostalgic whimsy but a characteristically clever Churchill gesture to rally British spirits in the face of the German onslaught. During England's darkest days in July 1940, Churchill posed with the famous American weapon during a visit to troops near Hartlepool. He sought to raise morale in anticipation of a feared German land invasion. Nazi propagandists claimed that the widely disseminated photo showed that the British leader was no better than an American Prohibition-era criminal.

Churchill, though, understood that he needed to provoke Britain's patriotism and martial spirit at a time when some of his countrymen were calling for peace talks with the Nazis. The tommy gun Churchill held was one of a small batch the U.S. shipped to England specifically for this purpose—to signal American support for the Allies, even before Franklin D. Roosevelt believed he had sufficient political support at home for U.S. entry into the war against Hitler. The British moved the imported tommy guns around their country so they could be photographed in the hands of troops and create the false impression that British forces were all outfitted with the potent American submachineguns.

Grip held a seven-round magazine.

▲ COLT MODEL 1911A1

Country: United States

Date: 1943

Barrel Length: 5in

Caliber: .45

An upgrade of the M1911. The U.S. military used variations of the M1911 until the family of handguns was replaced by the M9 Beretta in the 1980s.

▲ WEBLEY MARK 1 NAVY PISTOL

Country: Great Britain

Date: 1913

Barrel Length: 5in

Caliber: .455

Webley self-loaders were used as personal sidearms by British forces in both world wars.

World War II Pistols

JAPANESE PISTOLS HAD A REPUTATION FOR BEING UNRELIABLE; NOT SO THE COLT 1911, WHICH WAS THE STANDARD-ISSUE FIREARM FOR U.S. ARMED FORCES.

Armies on both sides of the conflict equipped their officer corps with self-loading, or semiautomatic, pistols such as the German Luger and Walther and the American 1911 designed by John Browning and manufactured by Colt. Handguns weren't accurate at any significant distance and were intended primarily as self-defense weapons for infantry commanders, tank crews, and pilots. On the whole, the pistols of World War II didn't feature any significant technological advances over their predecessors World War I.

United States
During World War II, U.S. forces continued to carry the trusted Colt 1911 .45-caliber pistol, familiar to movie goers from such films as *Saving Private Ryan* (1998). In one of the movie's climactic scenes, the mortally wounded Captain Miller (Tom Hanks) bravely, if futilely, fires his 1911 at an approaching German tank. Select British and American special forces also used the Browning HP 35 (Hi-Power), a highly regarded 9mm pistol manufactured in Belgium beginning in 1935 that was John Browning's final creation.

Great Britain
Many British officers and airmen continued to arm themselves with

High-ranking Nazis got the custom Walthers with eagle-stamped grips.

Carl Walther: Arming the Germans

Carl Walther (1858–1915) began making hunting rifles in 1886 in what was then the German state of Hesse (now Thuringia). In 1908, Walter's oldest son, Fritz, diversified into handguns, and by the late 1920s the Walther factory was manufacturing the Polizeipistole (PP), a police pistol, followed by the Polizeipistole Kriminalmodell (PPK), a smaller model designed for detectives. With the rise of the Nazi regime, the Walther family won a lucrative contract to replace the Luger with a 9mm version of the PP known as the P38, the standard German sidearm in World War II. For most of the war, the Walther company exploited slave labor provided by the Nazi regime. Allied forces eventually destroyed Walther's plants, but Fritz Walther retained his designs and restarted manufacturing in Ulm, West Germany, in 1953.

During the cold war, the Walther PP and PPK became globally popular double-action pistols and were widely imitated by other manufacturers. The pistol's cachet increased in the 1960s when Ian Fleming put a sleek Walther PPK in the hands of secret agent James Bond (who'd begun his globe-trotting career with a Beretta pistol). And Bond wasn't the only pillar of popular culture to prefer the Walther. Elvis Presley owned a sliver-plated PPK inscribed with the initials TCB for "taking care of business." Today, Smith & Wesson manufactures the PPK in the United States in cooperation with Walther Arms.

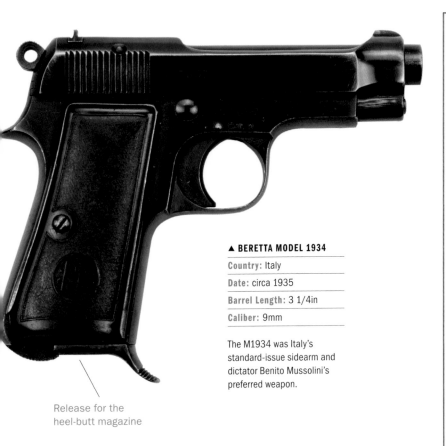

▲ BERETTA MODEL 1934

Country: Italy

Date: circa 1935

Barrel Length: 3 1/4in

Caliber: 9mm

The M1934 was Italy's standard-issue sidearm and dictator Benito Mussolini's preferred weapon.

Release for the heel-butt magazine

Webley Mark 4 and Enfield No. 2 Mark 1 revolvers as well as Smith & Wesson Model 10s. To prepare for a German ground invasion, British police and the Local Defense Volunteers were issued Ross rifles, Webley semiautomatics, and more than 20,000 U.S.-provided .32 Colts. British spies sometimes carried Welrod silenced pistols. But when it came to handguns, the British military generally stuck with revolvers.

Russia

The Russians carried a knockoff of the John Browning design for the 1911 called the Tula-Tokarev, or TT, a reference to the Soviet arsenal at Tula and to Feodor Tokarev, a former Czarist officer who later designed arms for the Communists. The eight-round weapon first introduced in 1933 has a Browning-style recoil-driven self-loading action.

Germany

The German army gradually replaced the Luger pistol with the highly regarded Walther P38, a military version of a 9mm police handgun developed by Carl Walther. The rugged P38's grip was made of Bakelite, an early form of industrial plastic. The standard handgun of Germany's Axis ally Italy was the Beretta M1934 9mm manufactured by the descendants of the early 16th-century Beretta family gunsmiths of Venice. The Beretta grip houses a nine-round magazine.

Japan

In contrast to the generally well-regarded German and Italian pistols, the Japanese armed officers and certain troops with semiautomatic handguns notorious for their unreliability. Named for Colonel Nambu Kirijo, Japan's leading gun designer, Nambu pistols frequently fired accidentally, because of defective cocking mechanisms, poor workmanship, or both. Allied bombing of Japanese factories late in the war further reduced the quality of Nambu handguns.

▲ WALTHER P38

Country: Germany

Date: 1938

Barrel length: 4 9/10in

Caliber: .35

This Walther replaced the Lugar PO8 as Germany's official military sidearm.

The TT-33 was produced through the mid 1950s.

▲ TULA-TOKAREV 33

Country: U.S.S.R.

Date: 1933

Barrel Length: 4 3/4in

Caliber: .30

A lighter-weight knockoff of Colt's Browning-designed M1911 pistol.

Novel toggle-action required the shooter to pull up, not back, to open the knee joint

Tapered barrels had varying lengths.

▲ LUGER 9MM

Country: Germany

Date: 1900–1945

Caliber: .35

Germans sometimes booby-trapped the Lugers of their fallen soldiers to kill souvenir-hunting Americans.

▲ REMINGTON RAND M1911A1 PISTOL

Country: United States

Date: 1942

Caliber: .45

Remington Rand, an office-supply company, made weapons and parts during the war years.

▲ ENFIELD NO. 2 MARK 1

Country: Great Britain

Date: 1926

Barrel Length: 5in

Caliber: .38

Produced by the Royal Small Arms Factory, the Enfield replaced the standard-issue Webley Mk4. But an acute arms shortage sent the Webley back to the battlefield.

▲ COLT POCKET HAMMERLESS PISTOL

Country: United States

Date: 1903

Barrel Length: 3 3/4in

Caliber: .32

The Colt hammerless was mainly used by government-service noncombatants.

▶FP-45 LIBERATOR

Country: United States

Date: 1942

Barrel Length: 4in

Caliber: .45

About 50,000 Liberators were dropped out of bombers into occupied Europe.

Not designed for repeat firing, Liberators were considered disposable.

Weapons of the Resistance

HOW POLISH, DANISH, FRENCH, ITALIAN, AND NORWEGIAN PARTISANS ARMED THEMSELVES.

Tubular barrel and receiver made from rolled steel

Although overwhelmingly outgunned by Nazi occupation forces, the resistance organizations of several European countries cobbled together armaments smuggled in by Allied forces, captured from the Germans, and in some cases, manufactured in underground workshops.

Great Britain

Designed and rushed into production in 1940, when Great Britain feared an imminent German invasion, the Sten submachinegun was originally intended to defend the beaches, fields, and streets of England. Produced by the millions, the Sten became one of the most recognizable British small arms of World War II and also a weapon that Allied forces smuggled to resistance forces in German-occupied regions. "Sten" is an acronym referring to its inventors, Reginald Shepherd and Harold Turpin, and the Enfield arms factory where they worked. The weapon held 32 rounds of 9mm ammunition and was accurate to only about 300 feet. Each all-metal Sten cost only about $10 to produce, compared to $200 for an American M1A1 Thompson submachinegun. The Allied military got what it paid for: The Sten was prone both to jamming and, if set down carelessly, discharging an entire magazine. Clever British troops turned the latter tendency to their advantage, tossing cocked and loaded Stens through a door or window. Upon impact, the guns would fire in all directions until empty—an effective way to slay Germans without storming a building. Polish, Danish, French, and Norwegian partisans all built do-it-yourself versions of the Sten and used them in their resistance movements.

▲ RADOM VIS PISTOL

Country: Poland

Date: 1936

Barrel Length: 4 3/4in

Caliber: 9mm

Insurgents secretly continued producing Poland's adopted service arm until 1945.

May 1944: Guerrillas in the Italian mountains.

French resisters in Montpellier on January 1, 1944.

▲ STEN SUBMACHINEGUN MARK I

Country: Great Britain

Date: 1941

Barrel Length: 7 1/2in

Caliber: .35

Poland

The Polish resistance produced the 9mm Vis pistol, also known as the Radom, a derivative of the American .45-caliber M1911. After the Germans relocated Polish gun factories to Austria, the resistance secretly resumed production from stolen parts and crudely fabricated components. Polish guerrillas also designed and made their own submachinegun, the Blyskawica, or "lightning" gun. These were loosely modeled on British-made Sten guns dropped into the country by the Allies. A more direct knockoff of the Sten, the Polski Sten, was made from nonmilitary material such as ordinary metal tubing and springs.

France

In addition to smuggled Sten submachineguns, the Maquis guerrilla groups relied on British-made Welrod suppressed assassin's pistols manufactured by the Inter-Services Research Bureau at Welwyn Garden City. The Maquis focused energetically on stealing firearms from the Germans, including Mauser rifles and carbines and the MP40 submachinegun. Of the latter, one French resistance fighter is said to have quipped: "They are as common as Parisian street hookers, and they get about as much action."

In the Air and at Sea

MILITARY SMALL ARMS ADAPTED WELL TO THE VARYING
REQUIREMENTS OF ALL THE U.S. ARMED FORCES.

Throughout the war, the Army Air Corps and the Marines modified small arms for their special needs. The Army Air Corps, for example, required "fixed mount" machineguns for the wings of fighters, while the Marines altered the Browning .30 caliber ANM2 with the stock from an M1 Garand. A pair of M2 machineguns was turned into an antiaircraft weapon by adding water-cooled sleeves over the barrels and shooting a "wall of lead" for enemy planes to fly into.

U.S. Marines prepared for an offensive on Iwo Jima in early 1945.

Royal Navy soldiers monitored their coast with a British-made Lewis machinegun in 1940.

This newly designed PT boat, outfitted with developing weaponry, didn't make it past the trial stage.

Increasingly sophisticated aircraft changed the rules of battle during World War II; a U.S. Marine Corps gunner on Guadalcanal Island.

In the Cause of Espionage

SMALL, PORTABLE AND OPTIMALLY QUIET, THESE ARMS
OFTEN COMBINED UNLIKELY FEATURES WITH LETHAL ENDS.

A built-in silencer dropped
the sound of the gunshot to
little more than a cough.

In World War I and World War II, both sides adapted existing firearms and developed new ones to suit the needs of spies, special forces, and saboteurs. Special-purposes weapons featured stealth, sound suppression, and portability. During World War II, the British Special Operations Executive and its American counterpart, the Office of Strategic Services (OSS), also supplied weapons to resistance groups in Nazi-occupied Europe, including the Liberator, an inexpensive single-use pistol dropped by airplane behind enemy lines.

▶ WEBLEY & SCOTT
MODEL 1911

Country: Great Britain

Date: 1911

Length: 6 1/4in

Caliber: .32

Single-action
trigger

▼ STINGER PEN GUN

Country: United States

Date: 1942

Length: 3 1/2in

Caliber: .22

The OSS instructions read: "It
can be fired from the palm of
the hand at a person sitting in a
room or passing in a crowd...and
can be distributed to patriots of
occupied countries."

Combination
revolver, knife, and
knuckleduster

◀ APACHE KNUCKLEDUSTER

Country: Belgium

Date: 1870s

Length: 5in

Caliber: .20

Named after a French street
gang who used these in the late
1800s and early 1900s.

Ten one-shot stingers were
packed in a moisture-proof
box for shipping.

▲ OSS HI-STANDARD

Country: United States

Date: 1942

Length: 12 1/2in

Caliber: .22

The Hartford Arms 1925 target pistol morphed into a spy gun 15 years later.

When baffles lining the barrel began to wear out, a combatant could plug a wad of gum into the barrel depression to help silence the shot.

▼ LE PROTECTOR PALM PISTOL

Country: France

Date: 1882

Barrel Length: 1 1/2in

Caliber: .32

One squeeze of a closed hand fired a bullet between two fingers.

▲ WELROD ASSASSINATOR

Country: Great Britain

Date: circa 1942

Barrel Length: 8 1/2in

Caliber: .32

To maintain deniability and secrecy, manufacturers refrained from putting their stamp on the pistol. The earlierst Welrod looked like a bicycle pump.

July 10, 1939

November 20, 1939

May 27, 1940

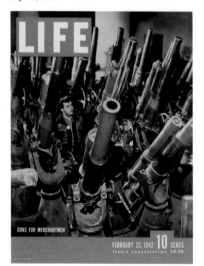

February 23, 1942

April 6, 1942

July 13, 1942

LIFE Covers the War's Guns

WEAPONS WERE A CORNERSTONE OF LIFE MAGAZINE'S
COVERAGE OF THE WAR, THE FRONT LINES, AND BEHIND THEM.

No other magazine covered World War II with the depth and breadth of LIFE. Twenty-one of the magazine's photographers spent 13,000 days outside the United States, often in combat zones. The images they sent home were searing and memorable, ranging from the rubble of the Battle of Britain to the sands and jungles of Guadalcanal. Covers featuring guns transmitted an especially powerful message.

June 5, 1944

July 27, 1940

October 28, 1940

December 29, 1941

September 7, 1942

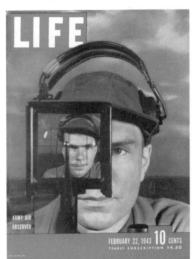

February 22, 1943

March 27, 1944

June 12, 1944

September 11, 1944

October 30, 1944

10 | MODERN TIMES, NEW MATERIALS

SINCE THE END OF WORLD WAR II, GUNMAKERS HAVE CREATED WEAPONS
THAT ARE LIGHTER, STURDIER, AND MORE ACCURATE.

U.S. Marines on patrol in Afghanistan. The soldier on the left carries an M249 SAW; the middle soldier has an M4 with an M203 grenade launcher; the soldier on the right carries an M4.

U.S. planes delivered food and supplies to Berlin throughout the Soviets' blockade of the city from 1948 to 1949.

The Cold War Confrontation

ANTAGONISM BETWEEN THE UNITED STATES AND THE SOVIET UNION HELPED
FOSTER THE DEVELOPMENT OF NEW TYPES OF WEAPONS.

Without drastically changing the basic mechanics of firearms, gun designers after World War II employed new materials and production methods to make guns that were lighter, more durable, and capable of greater firepower. Wood gave way to plastics; pressed metal parts replaced components milled from solid steel; magazine capacity increased and with it lethality.

Distinctive "families" of firearms began to develop based on the long cold war confrontation between the Soviet Union, with its signature AK-47, and the United States, which armed its troops with the M16 and its progeny. These two assault rifles saw heavy action in Vietnam, as well as in proxy wars elsewhere in Asia, Africa, and Latin America. Imitations—some legally licensed, others merely pirated—were produced in nations around the world. In the realm of handguns, meanwhile, beginning in the early 1980s, a large-capacity black plastic pistol designed by an obscure Austrian curtain-rod manufacturer named Gaston Glock revolutionized the market for military, law enforcement, and civilian sidearms.

Moving Forward From the Battlefield

The evolution of guns is inextricably intertwined with changing strategies on the battlefield, and to a lesser extent policing methods. Glancing back in time, it's clear that breech-loading repeating rifles transformed warfare in the late 19th century. Improved rifles enabled individual soldiers moving in irregular patterns to maintain sustained fire, undermining the advantages

From top left: The Berlin Wall under construction in 1961; Communist leaders gathered in Moscow on December 21,1949; President Harry Truman signed the NATO defense pact on April 4, 1949; In 1968, the Soviets paraded their latest intercontinental ballistic missiles through Red Square in Moscow.

of disciplined units operating in lockstep formation. In similar fashion, the greater accuracy and rapidity of fire associated with World War II–era self-loading rifles such as the M1 Garand heightened the effectiveness of individual combatants. By the end of World War II and in the years thereafter, the assault rifle, invented by the Germans and advanced by the Soviets, continued to accelerate the evolution of warfare.

No longer was the bulky crew-operated machinegun the only means of delivering sustained, high-volume fire. Beginning with German designs of the 1940s, assault weapons were light, portable, accurate to roughly 1,500 feet, and, when set to fully automatic mode, capable of firing as fast as 850 rounds in a minute or less. All the user had to do was keep the trigger depressed and the weapon aimed roughly at his foe.

In *The Gun*, an authoritative social history of the AK-47, journalist C.J. Chivers offers this description: "At a glance, the new rifle was in many ways peculiar, an oddity...Its components were simple, inelegant, and by Western standards, of seemingly workmanlike craftsmanship. The impression it created was the puzzling embodiment of a firearm compromise, a blend of design choices no existing Western army was willing yet to make... None of the Soviet Union's Cold War opponents had managed to conceive of, much less produce, a firearm of such firepower at such compact size... It was so reliable, even when soaked in bog water and coated in sand, that its Soviet testers had trouble making it jam."

By the late 1950s, the uncanny reliability of the Russian AK-47 made it deadly even in the hands of poorly trained fighters, including members of insurgencies, anticolonial forces, and terrorists. This further eroded the edge once enjoyed by disciplined regiments closely following a leader's commands. The late 20th century became the era of the assault rifle, and its dominance continued beyond into the new millennium.

▲ **AK-47**

Country: U.S.S.R.	
Date: circa 1954	
Barrel Length: 15 1/2in	
Caliber: 7.62mm	

This is the weapon of choice for more than 55 national armies and countless law-enforcement agencies and rebel groups worldwide.

The Father of the AK-47

RUSSIAN SOLDIER AND INVENTOR MIKHAIL KALASHNIKOV SET OUT TO BUILD A BETTER ASSAULT RIFLE. IT BECAME THE MOST INFLUENTIAL GUN OF THE 20TH CENTURY.

Mikhail Kalashnikov (1919–2013), an autodidact gun designer and the most influential small-arms innovator of the 20th century, expressed defensiveness and even regret about his greatest creation. But above all, he felt pride. Of the AK-47, the ubiquitous battlefield rifle, he said: "I created a weapon to defend the borders of my motherland. It's not my fault that it's being used where it shouldn't be. The politicians are more to blame for this."

A sickly child, Mikhail was born to a poor Siberian peasant family that later was deported to a rural village in Tomsk Oblast. He grew up tinkering with machinery, hunting with his father's old-fashioned rifle, and writing poetry—a literary pursuit he continued for most of his life. Conscripted into the Red Army during World War II, Kalashnikov became a mechanic, then a tank commander, and was wounded in the shoulder in the Battle of Bryansk in October 1941. During his recovery, he heard fellow soldier patients criticizing the standard-issue Soviet Mosin-Nagant rifle and audaciously decided to design a better one.

Upon his release from the hospital, Kalashnikov obtained an appointment to the Red Army's Central Scientific Rifle Firing Range, where he explored various ideas for a submachinegun and a gas-operated carbine similar to the highly regarded American M1 Garand. He eventually made his mark during a Soviet postwar competition by creating an assault rifle that outperformed the German MP44 Sturmgewehr. Kalashnikov called his prototype the Mikhtim, a combination of his first name and his patronymic, Timofeyevich. That initial model evolved into the Avtomat Kalashnikova Model 1947, or AK-47.

Explaining his thinking as an engineer, he said that as a young man he'd read that God Himself believed that "all that is too complex is unnecessary." Instead, "it is simple that is needed." This thinking inspired Kalashnikov's lifetime motto: "simple and reliable."

Defining Characteristics

The AK-47 is a selective-fire weapon, meaning that it can function in either semiautomatic (one round per trigger pull) or fully automatic mode. It is gas-operated and fires 7.62 x 39mm ammunition from a distinctive forward-curving, detachable 30-round magazine, sometimes referred to as a "banana clip." The Soviet army introduced the weapon in 1948 and officially adopted it as the standard-issue assault rifle the following year. Known as the "Kalash" to Russian soldiers, the AK-47 soon spread to the militaries of other members of the Soviet bloc, and from there to farther-

In designing the AK-47, Mikhail Kalashnikov wanted to make a selective-fire weapon that was highly reliable and user-friendly.

There are at least 100 million Kalashnikovs in circulation. Here, an Iraqi policeman trained to use the weapon in Jordan.

detachable cleaning rod

flung client states and guerrilla armies.

The gun's appeal was based on several basic characteristics: low production costs, simplicity of use, and durability under a variety of harsh conditions. In semiautomatic mode, the AK-47 can fire as rapidly as the shooter can pull the trigger and change magazines; in fully automatic mode, it can fire more than 600 rounds. Over the next six decades, an estimated 100 million Kalashnikov rifles and knockoff versions were manufactured internationally. "It was midsized in important measures— shorter than the infantry rifles it would displace but longer than the submachine guns that had been in service for 30 years," observed one

historian. "It fired a medium-powered cartridge, not powerful enough for long-range sniping duty, but with adequate energy to strike lethally and cause terrible wounds within the ranges at which almost all combat occurs." No 20th-century gun has had a broader influence.

Kalashnikov, who rose to the rank of chief Soviet weapon designer, described his creation as including the best features of the M1 Garand and the MP44 Sturmgewehr. "Before attempting to create something new," he once said, "it is vital to have a good appreciation of everything that already exists in this field."

The AK-47 has relatively few components and there are generous

clearances between moving parts, allowing the gun to function even after the buildup of residue and dirt. This reliability, however, limits the AK-47's precision. It is not a particularly accurate gun and isn't meant to be. Fired from the shoulder or hip, it emits a stream of bullets plenty deadly at short and intermediate distances.

Over time, the Soviet Union introduced improved versions of the Kalashnikov known as the AKM (M for modernized) and the AK-74, which accommodates 5.45mm ammunition. During the long cold war, the Soviets and the Chinese both shipped vast numbers of AK variants to allied anti-Western governments

Folding metal stock

◄ AK-74

Country: U.S.S.R.

Date: 1974

Barrel Length: 16 1/3in

Caliber: 5.45 x 39mm

The AK-74's smaller, lighter, high-velocity military cartridges allowed soldiers to carry more ammunition. It replaced the AKM as the standard Soviet assault rifle.

▲ AKM

Country: U.S.S.R.

Date: 1959

Barrel Length: 16 1/3in

Caliber: 7.62 x 39mm

A newly added folding shoulder stock gave soldiers the option of shortening the weapon by 10 inches.

and rebel groups around the world, fueling decades of conflict. The United States, in turn, armed its allies with costly select-fire automatic weapons, chiefly the M14 and M16.

Ongoing Influence

In the 1990s, after the fall of the Soviet empire, AK-47s and their descendants continued to proliferate, turning up in the arsenals of drug-trafficking organizations and extremists such as Al Qaeda and ISIS. In Russia, China, and parts of the developing world, the AK-47 retained a reputation associated with resistance to Western domination. All told, more than 55 armies throughout the world have adopted the AK, and its variants are

built in some 30 nations.

Kalashnikov the man became a military and cultural hero in his home country, appearing in public, his barrel chest festooned with military awards. The AK-47 did not, however, directly generate huge personal wealth for its inventor. He didn't own Izhmash, the gun's official manufacturer, which, in any event, didn't patent the weapon until the late 1990s. By that time, manufacturers the world over were churning out pirated AK designs, and Izhmash accounted for only 10 percent of global production.

Late in life, Kalashnikov did receive a 30 percent interest in a German marketing company run

by his grandson Igor that slapped the family name on such diverse products as knives, umbrellas, and even vodka. The elder Kalashnikov died in 2013 at the age of 94. In a letter written to the leader of the Russian Orthodox Church shortly before his death and published by the newspaper *Izvestia*, the gun pioneer asked what he plaintively called an "insoluble question": whether he was personally responsible for "the death of people."

Patriarch Kirill reportedly wrote back that Kalashnikov could rest easy. "When the weapon is used in defense of the Motherland, the Church supports its creators and the military which use it."

Into Korea

THE WORLD'S INABILITY TO UNITE NORTH AND
SOUTH RESULTED IN A BLOODY NEW WAR.

The clash over the Korean peninsula was the world's first military action between two nuclear powers, and for America, a critical effort to contain communism.

The conflict dated to the early 20th century, a time when Korea was annexed to Japan. But with the collapse of the Japanese empire at the end of World War II, Korea was left without a native government and the country was riven by competing political interests. Stepping in, the United States and the Soviet Union agreed to divide Korea along the 38th parallel for administrative purposes, but the arrangement quickly deteriorated when the two countries could not agree on a unification plan. Once the United Nations recognized an independent southern Korea, partisan warfare broke out. The conflict went global in 1950 after North Korea, aided by the Soviet Union, invaded South Korea, and the United Nations and the United States joined South Korea. Because of changes in military tactics, firearms innovation slowed, but the casualty rate for the three-year war was high. Nearly five million people died, more than half of whom were civilians.

U.S. troops (circa 1950) landed in an open field during the Korean War. Six decades later, 7,800 Americans are still unaccounted for.

Guns of Korea

THE CONFLICT WAS FOUGHT PRIMARILY WITH
SURPLUS WEAPONS FROM WORLD WAR II.

During the Korean conflict, both U.S.-led United Nations forces and their Communist opponents battled primarily with surplus World War II weapons. In the United States, the development of nuclear weapons and the notion that major ground wars would become a thing of the past influenced military planners to all but cease procurement of new or innovative infantry firearms. In Korea, Soviet, and Chinese factories supplied many of the weapons used by the North Korean People's Army and their Chinese backers.

▲ BROWNING M1917A1

Country: United States

Date: 1917–1937

Barrel Length: 24in

Caliber: .30

The last water-cooled Browning machinegun weighed more than 100 pounds with tripod, water, and ammunition.

Wraparound bottom plate supported the receiver.

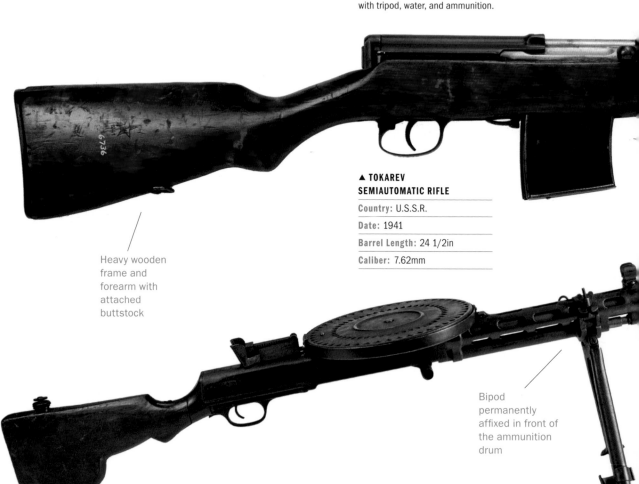

▲ TOKAREV
SEMIAUTOMATIC RIFLE

Country: U.S.S.R.

Date: 1941

Barrel Length: 24 1/2in

Caliber: 7.62mm

Heavy wooden frame and forearm with attached buttstock

Bipod permanently affixed in front of the ammunition drum

**▶ PPSH-41
SUBMACHINEGUN**

Country: U.S.S.R.

Date: 1942

Barrel Length: 10 1/2in

Caliber: 7.62mm

This model was easy to manufacture and reliable under most conditions.

Ten-round box magazine

**◀ DPM LIGHT
MACHINEGUN**

Country: U.S.S.R.

Date: 1936

Barrel Length: 24in

Caliber: 7.62mm

The DPM was designed to give a small infantry unit more sustained firepower than a rifle.

**▶ NAMBU
TYPE 14 PISTOL**

Country: Japan

Date: 1941

Barrel Length: 4 3/4in

Caliber: 8mm

The Nambu semiautomatic, which resembles a Luger, was the first Japanese service pistol.

A CONFLICT UNSPOOLS

The United States worried that the fighting in Korea could lead to a wider confrontation with Russia and China, or World War III.

1951 March: U.S. and ROK forces retook Seoul.

1950 June: North Korean troops crossed the 38th parallel, invading the Republic of Korea (ROK); President Harry Truman committed American forces to defend the South.

1950 July: North Korean People's Army took Suwon.

1951 January: American forces evacuated Seoul and withdrew from Inchon.

1950 | 1951 | 1952

1950 October: U.S. forces crossed the 38th parallel near Kaesong.

1951 April: Truman dismissed General MacArthur; Communist offensives failed.

1950 September: With American, United Nations, and Republic of Korea forces pushed back, General Douglas MacArthur launched the daring Inchon Invasion.

1951 July: Peace talks began at Kaesong.

1952 July: U.S. air attacks on Pyongyang.

1953 June: Peace talks resumed at Panmunjom.

| | | 1953 | | | | | | | | | | 1954 | | | | | | | | | | | | 1955 |

1953 April: The Battle of Pork Chop Hill was fought during armistice talks.

1953 July: Negotiators reached a peace accord; the 38th parallel was reset as the boundary between Communist North Korea and American-allied South Korea.

Arming for Vietnam

EUGENE STONER'S M16 BECAME THE
MILITARY'S STANDARD SERVICE RIFLE.

Although overshadowed by his Russian counterpart, Mikhail Kalashnikov, America's assault-rifle pioneer, Eugene Stoner (1922–1997), also deserves recognition as one of the most influential small-arms designers of the 20th century.

Born in Indiana and raised in southern California, Stoner served in the Marine Corps during World War II, handling aviation ordnance in the Pacific and northern China. He

continued in the aircraft equipment field after the war and gravitated toward firearms, becoming the chief engineer for gunmaker ArmaLite, a division of Fairchild Engine & Airplane Corp.

At ArmaLite, Stoner designed a series of prototype rifles, including the AR-5, a small survival rifle for downed pilots, which was adopted by the Air Force. He moved on to work on the AR-10, a lightweight select-fire

A special ops unit (at left) with AR-15 and M16 rifles; (top right) Montagnard soldiers led by a U.S. officer; (bottom right) during Operation Pegasus in 1968, American soldiers help South Vietnamese forces lift the siege of Khe Sanh.

infantry rifle designed to fire then-standard NATO 7.62mm ammunition. Recognized as a potential leap forward because of its maneuverability, the AR-10 nevertheless was passed over for a more conventional model that became the clunkier M14—essentially an improved select-fire M1 Garand with a 20-round magazine. (The AR-10 design was licensed to a Dutch firm that produced it for some years for sale to other militaries.)

Jungle Conditions

Intended as the U.S. military's answer to the AK-47, the M14 didn't perform well in the jungles of Vietnam in the early 1960s. American troops found it uncontrollable when set to full auto, and its 20-round magazine didn't contain enough rounds to sustain heavy fire in battle against the superior Russian design. These shortcomings prompted Pentagon officials to turn back to Stoner's

AR-10—the seed from which grew a large crop of American military and civilian assault-style rifles.

Designers who had worked with Stoner built on his idea to create the AR-15, which fired scaled-down .223 Remington rounds.

In 1963, Defense Secretary Robert McNamara decided that the AR-15's firepower made it preferable to the M14 and ordered the variant of Stoner's design into production as

Practical rate
of fire of 40 to
100 rounds per
minute

Accomodates a
variety of scopes
and sights

▲ AR-10

Country: Netherlands	
Date: circa 1959	
Barrel Length: 20in	
Caliber: 7.62mm	

A selective fire lever allowed
the user to choose automatic or
semiautomatic. The AR-10 was
quickly replaced by the AR-15.

Wood buttstock
eventually
replaced by plastic

the basic infantry weapon for all U.S.
services. McNamara was influenced
by reports from American special-
forces soldiers who tested prototype
AR-15s under extreme conditions in
Vietnam and found them effective.

Colt had bought the rights to
the AR-15 from ArmaLite and
thus benefited from the enormous
orders that poured in for what was
renamed the M16 standard Army
rifle. More streamlined than the M14,
the new model was made from steel,
aluminum, and industrial-strength
plastic. Its extreme lightness allowed
troops to carry more ammunition.
Initially, the M16 tended to jam
when exposed to the damp, dirty
conditions of jungle warfare—a
severe disadvantage when compared
to the practically jam-proof AK-47.
But after a series of modifications, the
American rifle gradually achieved
improved performance and won the
approval of most officers and rank-
and-file troops.

Stoner left ArmaLite in 1961 and
served as a consultant to Colt for
a time before moving on to other
employers, where he continued
to design assault rifles and
machineguns. None of them enjoyed
the influence of his AR-10 and AR-15.

▲ M16

Country: United States

Date: circa 1964

Barrel Length: 20in

Caliber: 5.56mm

The primary U.S. battle rifle during the Vietnam War, the M16 has been modified to make new versions like the M16A4 and the lighter, more compact M4.

Some soldiers complained that wooden bodies warped in jungle conditions, reducing accuracy.

▲ M14

Country: United States

Date: 1960

Barrel Length: 22in

Caliber: 7.62mm

Vietnam's early assault rifle was designed primarily for semi-automatic fire and had an effective range of 500 yards.

Other Guns of Vietnam

FROM THE COLT COMMANDO CARBINE TO THE
PPSH TYPE 50 SUBMACHINEGUN.

The premier proxy war of the cold war era, the Vietnam conflict pitted Communist North Vietnam, its Vietcong guerrilla allies in the South, and their Chinese and Soviet backers against anti-Communist South Vietnam, which was supported by the United States. American and South Vietnamese forces initially carried M14 rifles, soon to be replaced by the lighter and more accurate M16 assault rifle. Jamming problems with the M16 were addressed in 1968 with the issuance of the M16A1, which had a chrome-plated barrel. Communist forces were armed with Chinese- and Soviet-made guns, principally the ubiquitous AK-47, considered to be the most effective weapon of the war because of its ability to function reliably under the muddiest jungle conditions.

◀ **MAT 49 SUBMACHINEGUN**

Country:	France
Date:	1949
Barrel Length:	9in
Caliber:	.30

This was used by the French military in Korea, Laos, Cambodia, and Vietnam.

▲ **RPG 7 ANTITANK GRENADE LAUNCHER**

Country:	U.S.S.R.
Date:	1961
Length:	37 2/5in

This rocket-propelled grenade launcher was the most widely distributed of all Soviet antitank weapons.

Wooden heat shield

Twenty-round
magazine

▲ COLT COMMANDO CARBINE

Country: United States

Date: 1966

Barrel Length: 10in

Caliber: 5.56mm

Special Forces troops used this
carbine extensively throughout
the Vietnam War.

▲ PPSH TYPE 50
SUBMACHINEGUN

Country: China

Type 50 was a locally manufactured copy of the Soviet's
PPSh-41. It was nicknamed the
"burp" gun because of the sound
it made when fired.

Seventy-one–
round drum

A LONG JUNGLE WAR

After two decades of grueling combat, the conflict ended with Vietnam united under the control of the Communists.

1964 The Gulf of Tonkin incident, in which a U.S. destroyer exchanged shots with North Vietnamese torpedo boats, led to a congressional resolution giving President Lyndon Johnson the power to defend South Vietnam.

1954 Viet Minh forces overran the French command post at Dien Bien Phu, undermining French resolve to continue the First Indochina War.

1959 The North Vietnamese army created a supply route to guerrilla forces fighting in the South; the route along the Vietnamese-Cambodian border became known as the Ho Chi Minh Trail.

1968 January: North Vietnam's Tet Offensive, where 37,000 Vietcong were killed, was a fiasco for the Communists; but the heavy fighting cost the war effort public support in America.

| 1955 | | 1960 | | 1965 | |

1962 Operation Chopper marked the first U.S. Army combat mission against the Vietcong as American helicopter pilots ferried South Vietnamese soldiers into battle.

1961 President John F. Kennedy ordered more U.S. military assistance for the South Vietnamese government in its war against the Vietcong.

1966 American forces reached 385,000 soldiers, plus 60,000 sailors offshore; Vietcong ranks swelled to more than 280,000.

1969 January: President Richard Nixon took office, promising "peace with honor."

1974 Nixon resigned amid scandal in Washington, as North Vietnamese captured territory in violation of Paris Peace Accords.

1975 North Vietnamese offensives sent the South Vietnamese army reeling. In April, the last two American troops were killed; the U.S. embassy in Saigon was abandoned, and North Vietnamese tanks rolled into the capital city of the South.

| 1970 | 1975 | 1980 |

1968 March: The My Lai massacre by American troops raised questions at home about the conduct of the war.

1969 June: Nixon announced the beginning of U.S. troop withdrawals.

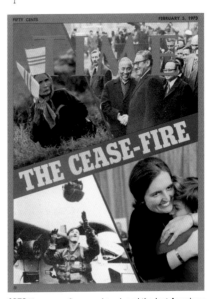

1973 The cease-fire was signed, and the last American combat troops left South Vietnam; 58,000 Americans had died, with more than 1,000 more missing in action.

Gaston Glock exploited contacts in the Austrian defense ministry to sell his pistol.

From Curtain Rods to the "Pistol of the Future"

AUSTRIAN ENGINEER GASTON GLOCK FASHIONED A NEW
KIND OF GUN FROM INJECTION-MOLDED PLASTIC.

An undistinguished Austrian engineer with no background in firearms, Gaston Glock (born 1929) ran a radiator plant in suburban Vienna. On the side, he and his wife, Helga, manufactured curtain rods, brass fittings, and bayonets in his garage. They use a secondhand Russian metal press, which Helga oversaw during the day while Gaston worked at the factory.

In 1980, Gaston Glock learned that the Austrian army desired a new sidearm to replace the antiquated Walther P38 of World War II vintage. Steyr, Austria's premier arms maker since the mid-1880s, offered an ungainly update that tended to misfire. Glock, who had business contacts in the defense ministry, saw an opportunity. He studied the best pistols available and consulted with leading European firearm experts. His goal, he later explained, was to produce "a pistol of the future."

The Austrian army sought a pistol that was light, durable, and capable of holding more than the eight rounds the Walther accommodated. Glock fabricated a frame from an injection-molded plastic known as polymer, a featherweight material that proved remarkably strong and corrosion-resistant. In the evenings he tested crude early versions in a basement firing range beneath his suburban home. He shot alone, using only his left hand, so that if the gun blew up he would still have his right to do mechanical drawings.

In 1981, Glock filed for an Austrian patent—his 17th, so he called the gun the Glock 17. Coincidentally, it could store 17 rounds in its magazine, with an 18th in the chamber. In competitive trials in 1982, the Glock defeated models made by Steyr and four other well-known European arms manufacturers. The Austrian military ordered 20,000 Glock 17s. Suddenly, Gaston Glock had to build a factory, for he found himself in the gun business.

The squared-off Glock pistol was built for efficiency—not unlike the AK-47 introduced in the late 1940s by Soviet assault weapon pioneer Mikhail Kalashnikov. The Glock lacked the blued-steel frame and polished wooden grips of a classic American revolver. Its black matte finish seemed homely to many gun lovers. It had relatively few parts (like the Kalashnikov) and rarely jammed.

Glock knew that selling the pistol in Europe alone would limit his commercial possibilities. He hired an ambitious Austrian-American marketer named Karl Walter who had a plan for entering the U.S. market: "Where there really is money to be made," Walter predicted," is to convert U.S. police departments from revolvers to pistols." This proved prescient.

Since the 19th century, when the Colt Peacemaker became known as "the gun that won the West," Americans had preferred revolvers.

Glock 17 centerfire self-loading pistol

Continental Europeans, by contrast, favored pistols, also known as semiautomatics, with spring-loaded magazines that held more rounds and allowed for faster reloading. "I was astonished that this modern country still hung around with revolvers," Walter said years later, referring to the United States.

They made a complementary pair. Glock, the reticent engineer, unfamiliar with American tastes in guns or anything else, had a breakthrough product to sell. Walter, the garrulous expat, had valuable connections in the world's richest gun market. In 1985, Walter set up Glock's American subsidiary in a small warehouse-and-office complex near the Atlanta airport in Smyrna, Georgia. A year later, in the sort of coincidence from which fortunes are made, America's police collectively decided they needed a new handgun.

With violent, cocaine-driven crime on the rise, police officials saw themselves as outgunned. There was little statistical support for this; the typical police gunfight at the time involved the firing of two to three rounds by the cops—well within the capacity of a Smith & Wesson six-shot revolver. But in several notorious

The polymer frame is stronger than aluminum or steel, yet lighter than both.

▲ GLOCK 17

Country:	Austria
Date:	1982
Barrel Length:	4 1/2in
Caliber:	9mm

The 17 is used by law enforcement around the globe.

▶ GLOCK 23

Country:	Austria
Date:	1990
Barrel Length:	4in
Caliber:	.40

This easily concealable compact Glock packs 13 rounds.

incidents, including a shoot-out in Miami in April 1986 that left two FBI agents dead, criminals deployed more firepower than the law enforcers. "Although the revolver served the FBI well for several decades, it became quite evident that major changes were critical to the well-being of our agents and American citizens," FBI director William S. Sessions said after the Miami bloodshed.

In late 1986 the Miami police department ordered 1,100 Glock pistols, followed closely by Dallas, San Francisco, and others. "It's the wave of the future," said the chief in Minneapolis, who authorized Glocks for his officers. In December 1986, Curtiss Spanos, a policeman in Howard County, Maryland, fired 16 rounds in a 30-minute pursuit of two armed robbery suspects. "There would be two dead officers if I didn't have the 9mm gun," Spanos told *The Washington Post*. That kind of endorsement was something all the marketing dollars in the world could not buy. New York City at first banned the Glock by name, fearing it would be exploited by terrorists.

Then, in September 1988, the Associated Press reported that New York police commissioner Benjamin Ward was carrying a Glock 17 beneath his suit jacket. The *New York Post* ran this punning headline: TOP COP WARDS OFF BAN ON SUPER GUN. The NYPD soon dropped its ban on the Austrian pistol and began equipping its officers with the import.

Hollywood gave Glock another boost. In *Die Hard 2: Die Harder*, released on July 4, 1990, mercenary terrorists swarmed the big screen armed with Austrian pistols. The

Screen Shot

TV shows and movies have helped make the boxy black Glock part of American popular culture.

Agent Starling (Julianne Moore) in *Hannibal*

Ethan Renner (Kevin Costner) in *Three Days to Kill*

Samuel Gerard (Tommy Lee Jones) in *U.S. Marshals*

Law & Order detectives Tutuola (Ice-T) and Benson (Mariska Hargitay)

A Glock Deconstructed
Clockwise from top: steel slide, magazine tube, polymer grip, and receiver. Center: recoil spring and steel barrel.

hero, played by Bruce Willis (who carried a Beretta), at one point yelled at an airport police captain: "That punk pulled a Glock 7 on me! You know what that is? It's a porcelain gun made in Germany. It doesn't show up on your airport X-ray machines, and it costs more than you make here in a month."

It didn't matter that everything Willis' character said was inaccurate: The Glock was plastic, not porcelain; Austrian, not German. Even the model was wrong, but the Glock had entered American popular culture.

It became a lyric for rappers, the handgun carried by police characters on *Law & Order*, a brand name that came to stand for a product category.

Glock responded by designing and marketing a new generation of smaller pistols whose clips held 10 or fewer rounds—weapons the maker dubbed "Pocket Rockets." In 1995 the company introduced the Glock 26 and Glock 27 in 9mm and .40 caliber, respectively. The barrel and grip of the new models were an inch shorter than standard Glocks, but the ammunition was just as powerful.

Contemporary Assault Rifles

DESIGNERS TRY NEW CONFIGURATIONS, SOME MORE SUCCESSFUL THAN OTHERS.

While the United States and Russia have refined the basic assault rifle platforms—the M16 and AK-47, respectively—other countries have introduced the so-called "bullpup" configuration. An automatic bullpup rifle houses the bolt and recoil components in an enlarged butt, allowing the magazine to be positioned behind the trigger. This makes the bullpup more compact and reduces "muzzle rise," the tendency of assault rifles to jerk upward while firing. With the recoil mechanism in the rifle butt, more energy gets transferred to the shooter's body, allowing him, in theory, to hold the weapon steadier.

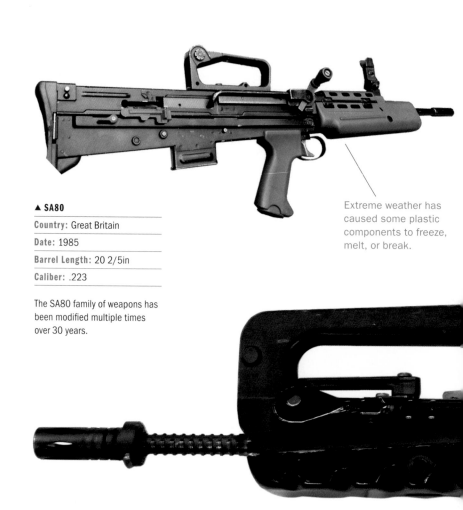

▲ **SA80**

Country: Great Britain

Date: 1985

Barrel Length: 20 2/5in

Caliber: .223

The SA80 family of weapons has been modified multiple times over 30 years.

Extreme weather has caused some plastic components to freeze, melt, or break.

Barrel grip

Can be fitted with an under barrel module to fire tear gas or grenades

▲ FABRIQUE NATIONALE F2000

Country: Belgium

Date: 2011

Barrel Length: 15 3/4in

Caliber: .223

▲ FAMAS F1

Country: France

Date: 1978

Barrel Length: 19 1/5in

Caliber: .223

Called "the bugle" because of its shape, the French standard-issue Famas was first used in 1981 in Kuwait during Operation Desert Storm.

◀ STEYR AUG A3M1

Country: Austria

Date: 1978

Caliber: .223

This 2014 bullpup Steyr was manufactured in Alabama.

Twenty-five round magazine

Arming the Navy SEAL Team

SOME WEAPONS CAN PENETRATE 20 LAYERS OF KEVLAR.

The U.S. Navy's Sea, Air, Land units, known SEAL teams, are one of the military's main special operations forces. With their roots in underwater demolition during World War II, SEAL teams are trained to operate in all environments and have played crucial—if generally top secret—roles in post-9/11 military activities in Afghanistan and Iraq. SEAL team members carried out the raid in Pakistan in 2011 that resulted in the death of Osama bin Laden, founder of the Islamic terrorist group Al Qaeda and architect of the 9/11 attacks on the United States. The weapons and gear SEAL team members carry vary from mission to mission, but these are some of the basics often used by the Navy's premier warriors.

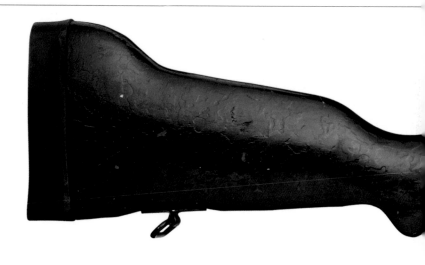

▲ **REMINGTON 870**

Country: United States

Date: 1951

Variants of the 12-gauge Remington 870 shotgun have been used by U.S. special operations forces for decades.

▲ **SIG-SAUER P226**

Country: Germany and United States

Date: 1984

Barrel Length: 4 4/5in

Caliber: 9mm

The aluminum-alloy pistol comes in a variety of calibers.

▲ M79 GRENADE LAUNCHER

Country: United States

Date: 1961

Barrel Length: 29in

Caliber: 40mm

This Vietnam-era weapon has been used during the Iraq war to explode suspected road bombs. It can hit a target from 380 yards.

▶ HECKLER & KOCH MP7A1

Country: Germany

Date: circa 2003

Barrel Length: 7in

Caliber: 4.6 x 30mm

Designed as a personal defense weapon, the MP7 can penetrate 20 layers of Kevlar from 220 yards.

Has a very high rate of fire: 950 rounds per minute

40mm grenade launcher

▲ M4A1 CARBINE

Country: United States

Date: 1994

Barrel Length: 14 1/2in

Caliber: .223

An Army-wide modification of nearly 500,000 M4s into M4A1s started in 2014.

Parting Shot

The monster gun of Tanjore, with a barrel measuring 24 feet, 5 inches long, was photographed in 1858 by Linnaeus Tripe in India. According to local lore, the cannon was fired only once and it took 40 minutes for a long trail of powder to reach the gun and ignite. "The sound, it seems, was as if Mount Meru had exploded…" Tripe wrote.

INDEX

PHOTO CREDITS

FRONT COVER From top: courtesy of Thomas del Mar Ltd.; Bryan Helm/ Galleries/Corbis; Nikreates/Alamy; (51.441, detail) The Walter's Art Museum, Baltimore BACK COVER From top: IWM/ Getty Images; Oleg Zabielin/Alamy; photo used with permission of Browning TITLE PAGE p.1: Herbert Gehr/The Life Picture Collection/Getty Images

p. 2: Chronicle/Alamy; (RAL.08455) ©Royal Armouries; Mary Evans Picture Library/Alamy; Corbis; Connecticut State Library; p. 3: Matthew Brady/Buyenlarge/ Getty Images; Edward S. Curtis/ Buyenlarge/Getty Images; FPG/Hulton Archive/Getty Images; Louis R. Lowry/U.S. Marine Corps; Oleg Zabielin/Alamy; p. 4: Lordprice Collection/Alamy

1: BLACK POWDER, ALCHEMY, AND BOMBARDS

pp. 6-7: RMN-Grand Palais/Art Resource, NY; pp. 8-9: Private Collection/©Look and Learn/Bridgeman Images; pp. 10-11: From left: ©Governing Body of Christ Church, Oxford; The Art Archive at Art Resource NY; Naval History and Heritage Command; pp. 12-13: clockwise from top left: age fotostock/Alamy; (XIX.164) ©Royal Armouries; (XIX.169) ©Royal Armouries; Greenshed/Wikimedia Commons; Musee de l'Armee/Dist. RMN-Grand Palais/ Art Resource NY; pp. 14-15: From top: North Wind Picture Archives; (XXI.3748) ©Royal Armouries; Musee de l'Armee/ Dist. RMN-Grand Palais/Art Resource NY; Public Domain/Wujing Zongyao; pp. 16-17: Clockwise from top: (XII.11787) ©Royal Armouries; NRA Museums; Musee de l'Armee/Dist.RMN-Grand Palais/ Art Resource, NY; (XXVIF.232) ©Royal Armouries; Public Domain/Wikipedia; The Metropolitan Museum of Art, Image source: Art Resource, NY

2: MATCHLOCKS AND MUSKETS

pp. 18-19: courtesy of Wellcome Library; pp. 20-21: NRA Museums (2); p. 22: PHAS/Getty Images; p. 23: From top: courtesy of Thomas del Mar Ltd; Imagno/ Getty Images; DEA/G. Dali Orti/Getty Images; pp.24-26: from top: (XXVIF.50) ©Royal Armouries; (XII.35) ©Royal Armouries; courtesy Thomas del Mar

(2); (X11.5315) ©Royal Armouries; pp.26-27: Yale Center for British Art, Gift of Paul Mellon, USA/In memory of his friend James Cox Brady, Class of 1929/ Bridgeman Images; pp. 28-29: From top: (XII.10) ©Royal Armouries (2); (XII.63) ©Royal Armouries; Top, The Metropolitan Museum of Art, Image source: Art Resource, NY; Bottom: Armed Forces History, NMAH, Smithsonian Institution

3: AN ERA OF EXPERIMENTATION

pp. 30-31: Interfoto/Alamy; pp. 32-33: NRA Museums (2); pp. 34-35: From left: Science Source; (XIII.48) ©Royal Armouries; DEA/G. Nimatallah/Getty Images; PHAS/Getty Images; pp. 36-37 From top: (XII.3754) ©Royal Armouries (2); Cleveland Museum of Art, OH, USA / Gift of Mr. and Mrs. Lewis R. Schilling/ Bridgeman Images; (XII.1551) ©Royal Armouries (2); pp. 38-39: (XII.732) ©Royal Armouries; (XII.1074) ©Royal Armouries; pp. 40–41 Clockwise from top: (XII.10250); (XII.1079); (XII.1781); (XII.1256)©Royal Armouries (4); pp. 42-43 Clockwise from top: (XIV.4) ©Royal Armouries; The Metropolitian Museum, Image source: Art Resource, NY; (XIV.6); (XIV.13); (XIV.23) ©Royal Armouries (3); pp. 44-45: From top: (XII.3513) ©Royal Armouries (2); (XII.5079) ©Royal Armouries; pp. 46-47: top: (XII1743) ©Royal Armouries; bottom: Hulton Archive/Getty Images; pp. 48-49: From top: (XII476) ©Royal Armouries; courtesy Thomas del Mar Ltd; (XII.3091) ©Royal Armouries; (XII.1692) ©Royal Armouries; (XII.1844) ©Royal Armouries; pp. 50-51: from top: (XII.3101) ©Royal Armouries; Cleveland Museum of Art, OH, USA /Gift of David S. Ingalls/Bridgeman Images; (XII.1885), (XII.3141) ©Royal Armouries (2); pp. 52-53: Clockwise from top: (XII.1728) ©Royal Armouries; courtesy of Thomas del Mar Ltd (2); pp. 54-55: from top: (XII.284) ©Royal Armouries; (XII.5705) ©Royal Armouries; (XII.1770) ©Royal Armouries; XII.2653/ Royal Armouries; pp. 56-57: From top: (XII.1549) ,(XII1278), (XII.10479) ©Royal Armouries (3); pp. 58-59: From top: The Metropolitan Museum of Art, Image source: Art Resource, NY; (XII1279) ©Royal Armouries (2); (XXVIF.6) ©Royal Armouries

4: COMING TO AMERICA

pp. 60-61: Princeton University Art Museum/Art Resource, NY; pp. 62-63: L – R: Corbis; NRA Museums (2); pp. 64-65: From top: MPI/Getty Images; Armed Forces History, NMAH, Smithsonian Institution; MPI/Getty Images; Hulton Archive/Getty Images; pp. 66-67: Top, L-R: Hulton Archive/Getty Images; Stocktrek Images/ Getty Images; Hulton Archive/Getty Images; courtesy Springfield Armory NHS, US NPS; William Smith/AP; Bottom, L-R: courtesy Springfield Armory NHS, US NPS; Library of Congress; (SPAR 4068) courtesy of Springfield Armory NHS, US NPS; Everett Collection; pp. 68-69: From top: (SPAR 933), (SPAR 2410), (SPAR 4068), (SPAR 3345), (SPAR 3444) courtesy Springfield Armory NHS, US NPS (5)

5: THE ROAD TO THE REVOLVER

pp. 70-71: courtesy Connecticut State Library; pp.72-73: (RAL.03725) ©Royal Armouries (2); pp. 74-75: From top: (XII.310), (XII.1411), (XII.9605), (XII8387) ©Royal Armouries (4) pp.76-77: From top: (XII.1419), (XII.713) ©Royal Armouries (2), (XII.1760) ©Royal Armouries (2), (XXVIF.216), (XII.680) ©Royal Armouries (2); pp.78-79": Clockwise from top left: NRA Museums, (XII.4154), (XII.1188), (PR.4972),(PR.10333) ©Royal Armouries (4); p. 80: (PR.2336)©Royal Armouries; p. 81: GL Archive/Alamy; p. 82: courtesy Connecticut State Library; p. 83: Don Troiani/Museum of Connecticut History/ Corbis; p. 84: Library of Congress; p. 85: Clockwise from top left: Library of Congress; courtesy Connecticut State Library; NRA Museums; pp. 86-87: Top, L-R: Corbis; US Patent and Trademark Office; Library of Congress; From the collection of the Indiana State Museum and Historic Sites; Library of Congress; Kean Collection/Getty Images; Bottom: courtesy of Connecticut State Library (3); pp. 88-89: Clockwise from top left: The Board of Trustees of the Armouries/ Heritage-Images/The Image Works ; Don Troiani/Museum of Connecticut History/ Corbis; The Board of Trustees of the Armouries/Heritage-Images/The Image Works; Don Troiani/The Museum of

Connecticut History /Corbis; pp.90-91: Don Troiani/The Museum of Connecticut History/Corbis (4); pp. 92-93: Left: NRA Museums; Right: L-R: ullstein bild via Getty Images; Everett Collection, Pictorial Parade/Getty Images; p. 94: The Metropolitan Museum, Image source: Art Resource, NY; p. 95 Top: NRA Museums; Bottom: (X11.5129) ©Royal Armouries; pp. 96-97: From top: (PR.2311), (PR.3471) ©Royal Armouries ((2), (XII.2924) ©Royal Armouries (2)

6: THE CIVIL WAR AND THE RISE OF THE RIFLE

pp. 98-99: Library of Congress; p. 100: SPAR 2410/courtesy Springfield Armory NHS, US NPS; p. 101: Library of Congress; pp. 102-103: From top: Armed Forces History, NMAH, Smithsonian Institution; Granger Collection; NRA Museums; pp. 104-105 From top: (XII.2587) ©Royal Armouries; NRA Museums (4); pp. 106-107: Library of Congress (16); p. 108: Library of Congress; p. 109: Clockwise from top left: Corbis; Library of Congress; Armed Forces History, NMAH, Smithsonian Institution; p. 110: Windsor Historical Society; p. 11: From top: Windsor Historical Society; (XII.2690) ©Royal Armouries (3); pp. 112 - 113: From top: Armed Forces History, NMAH, Smithsonian Institution; (XII.3575) ©Royal Armouries; NRA Museums; pp.114-115: From top: Library of Congress; NRA Museums (2); pp. 116-117: From top: NRA Museums; Armed Forces History, NMAH, Smithsonian Institution (3); pp. 118-119: Library of Congress (16); pp. 120-121: Top row: Boston Athenaeum; Library of Congress (7); Bottom row: Library of Congress (7); p. 122: Armed Forces History, NMAH, Smithsonian Institution; p. 123: Science Source/Getty Images

7: FIREARMS AND THE WILD WEST

pp. 124-125: Library of Congress; pp. 126-127: (XII.11119) ©Royal Armouries (2); p. 128: From top: NRA Museums; (PR.11076) ©Royal Armouries; NRA Museums; p. 129: Hulton Archive/Getty Images; MCT/Getty Images; p.130: Top: Getty Images; Bottom: Library of Congress; p. 131 Library of Congress

(4); p. 132: Underwood Archives/Getty Images; p. 133: NRA Museums (4); pp. 134-135: Clockwise from top left: NRA Museums; American Stock/Getty Images; Mark Leffingwell/Reuters/Corbis; NRA Museums; Kean Collection/Getty Images; pp. 136-137: Clockwise from top: Alamy; NRA Museums, Don Troiani/Corbis; Library of Congress; Bettmann/Corbis; Granger Collection; p. 138: Library of Congress; p. 139: Clockwise from top left: Wyoming State Archives; Mansell Collection/Time & Life Pictures; Helen H. Richardson/The Denver Post/Getty Images; p. 140: Library of Congress; p. 141: Clockwise from top left: MPI/Getty Images; ullstein bild/Getty Images; Matt Champlin/Getty Images; pp. 142-143: From top: (XII.1912) ©Royal Armouries; (SPAR 995) courtesy Springfield Armory NHS, US NPS; NRA Museums; p. 144: Clockwise from top left: Library of Congress (2); Don Troiani/ Museum of Connecticut History/Corbis; p.145: Top: Underwood Archives/Getty Images; Bottom: 20th Century Fox/Getty Images; pp. 146-147: Top row: Kansas State Historical Society; Kean Collection/ Getty Images; MPI/Getty Images; The New York Historical Society/Getty Images; Peter Bischoff/Getty Images; C.S. Fly/Arizona Historical Society; Library of Congress; MPI/Getty Images; Bottom row: Library of Congress; Universal History Archive/Getty Images; Crary Pullen; Library of Congress; Hulton Archive/Getty Images; Cramers Art Rooms of Cherryvale, KS/Wikimedia

8: WORLD WAR I AND
THE INDUSTRIALIZED WARFARE
p.148-149: US Army Signal Corps; pp. 150-151: From top: (SPAR 4068), (SPAR 4305) courtesy Springfield Armory NHS, US NPS (2); Pictorial Parade/Getty Images; pp. 152-153: From top: NRA Museums; (SPAR 4230) courtesy Springfield Armory NHS, US NPS; courtesy of the Waterloo Region Hall of Fame; pp. 154-155: Top row, L - R: AP (2); Library of Congress, Corbis (2); Popperfoto/Getty Images; Bottom row: Mansell Collection/Time & Life Pictures; Corbis; Mansell Collection/Time & Life Pictures; AP; Print Collector/Getty Images; AP; pp.156-157: (SPAR 4290) courtesy Springfield Armory NHS, US NPS; NRA Museums; (SPAR 5833), (SPAR 728)

courtesy Springfield Armory NHS, US NPS (2); pp. 158-159: Clockwise from top: NRA Museums (2); Peter Dazeley/Getty Images; Interfoto/Alamy; Granger Collection; pp. 160-161: From top left: Andrew Chittock/ Stocktrek Images/Getty Images; NRA Museums (3); p. 162: (PR.114) ©Royal Armouries; p.163 Science & Society Library/Getty Images; pp. 164-165: Clockwise from top left: (PR.7289) ©Royal Armouries; Library of Congress; Getty Images; (PR.7098) ©Royal Armouries; pp.166-167: Clockwise from top: (PR.7076); (PR. 189); (PR. 110) ©Royal Armouries (3); p.168 (PR.2218) ©Royal Armouries; p. 169: From top: (SPAR 1999) courtesy Springfield Armory NHS, US NPS; (XII.3732) ©Royal Armouries; p. 170-171: NRA Museums (6); 172-173: Clockwise from top left: photo used with permission of Browning; US Army; Library of Congress; photo used with permission of Browning; Robert Hunt Library/Mary Evans/The Image Works; NRA Museums; photo used with permission of Browning; p. 174: Top: Photo 12/UIG/Getty Images; Bottom: Maurice-Louis Branger/Roger Viollet/Getty Images; p. 175: From top: Jacques Boyer/ Roger Viollet/Getty Images; Hulton Archive/ Getty Images; ullstein bild/Getty Images; Universal History Archive/Getty Images; Bottom right: AP; p. 176: Top: Archive Photos/Getty Images; Bottom: Everett Collection; p. 177: Clockwise from top left: Alamy; Everett Collection; (2); p. 178: Left: AP; Right: ullstein bild/Getty Images; p. 179: Clockwise from top left: Wikipedia; Peter Stackpole/Time & Life Pictures/Getty Images; New York Daily News/Getty Images; Santi Visalli/Getty Images; pp. 180-181: Clockwise from left: Chicago Tribune/Getty Images; Chicago History Museum/Getty Images; Hulton Archive/Getty Images; Corbis; Alamy; Keystone-France/Gamma-Keystone/Getty Images

9: WORLD WAR II:
A GREAT GENERATION OF GUNS
pp. 182-183: W. Eugene Smith/Life Picture Collection/Getty Images; pp. 184-185: Clockwise from top left: National Archives; US Navy; Margaret Bourke White/Life Picture Collection/Getty Images; U.S. Coast Guard; p. 186: Clockwise from top left: Universal History Archive/Getty Images; AP

(3); Corbis; p. 187: Top: AP (6); Bottom: L-R: AP (3); Bottom right: Library of Congress; pp. 188-189: From top: (SPAR 3444), (SPAR759) courtesy Springfield Armory NHS, US NPS (2); (PR.10338) ©Royal Armouries; pp.190-191: From top: (SPAR 5820) courtesy Springfield Armory NHS, US NPS; NRA Museums; Armed Forces History, NMAH, Smithsonian Institution; Garand: courtesy Springfield Armory NHS, US, NPS; pp. 192-193: From top: (PR.1019) ©Royal Armouries; Armed Forces History, NMAH, Smithsonian Institution; (SPAR 1586), (SPAR 1571) courtesy Springfield Armory NHS, US, NPS (2); Armed Forces History, NMAH, Smithsonian Institution; pp. 194-195: From top: Andrew Chittock/Stocktrek Images/Getty Images; (SPAR 20) courtesy Springfield Armory NHS, US NPS; Andrew Chittock/Stocktrek Images/Getty Images (2); p. 196: (SPAR 1544) courtesy Springfield Armory NHS, US NPS; Armed Forces History, NMAH, Smithsonian Institution; p. 197: Library of Congress; pp. 198-199: From top: (SPAR 818), (SPAR 2762), (SPAR 1267) courtesy Springfield Armory NHS, US NPS (3); pp 200-201: Clockwise from top left: New York Daily News/Getty Images; Armed Forces History, NMAH, Smithsonian Institution; Bob Landry/ Life Picture Collection/Getty Images; IWM/Getty Images; Archive Photos/Getty Images; pp. 202: (SPAR 8827), (SPAR 1912) courtesy Springfield Armory NHS, US NPS (2); p. 203: Left: (SPAR 2086) courtesy Springfield Armory NHS, US NPS; Right: (PR.12124) ©Royal Armouries; pp. 204-205: Clockwise from top left: Andrew Chittock/Stocktrek Images/Getty Images; Corbis; AP (3); Gary Ombler/Getty Images; pp. 206-207: Clockwise from top left: (XII.8288) ©Royal Armouries; (SPAR 1043) courtesy Springfield Armory NHS, US NPS; Getty Images (2); (PR.7567) ©Royal Armouries; p. 208: From top: US Navy; IWM/Getty Images; p. 209: Clockwise from top: US Navy; AP; US Air Force; AP; pp. 210-211: Clockwise from top: (PR.4613) ©Royal Armouries; (SPAR 1520) courtesy Springfield Armory NHS, US NPS; (PR.11401), (PR.6735), (PR4717), (PR.13026) ©Royal Armouries (4); pp. 212-213: courtesy of TIME Inc.

10: MODERN TIMES, NEW MATERIALS
pp. 214-215: Robert Nickelsberg, p. 216: Walter Sanders/Life Picture Collection/Getty Images; p. 217: Clockwise from top left: Keystone-France/Getty Images; Sovfoto/ Getty Images; MPI/Getty Images; SVF2/ Getty Images; p. 218: (SPAR 772) courtesy Springfield Armory NHS, US NPS; p. 219: Heritage Images/Getty Images; p. 220: Scott Olson/Getty Images; zim286/Getty Images; p. 221: zim286/Getty Images; pp. 222-223: Hulton Archive/Getty Images; pp. 224-225: From top: (SPAR 3075), (SPAR 1594), (SPAR 5826), (SPAR 1051). (SPAR 2617) courtesy Springfield Armory NHS, US NPS; (5); pp. 226-227: Top row: Keystone/ Getty Images; AFP/Getty Images; Keystone/ Getty Images; MPI/Getty Images; Bottom row: Carl Mydans/Life Picture Collection/ Getty Images; Photo12/UIG/Getty Images; Authenticated News/Archive Photos/Getty Images; Central Press/Getty Images; 228: MILpictures by Tom Weber/Getty Images; p. 229: Top: Larry Burrows/Life Picture Collection/Getty Images (2); pp. 230-231: (SPAR 3289), (SPAR 1371), (SPAR 3345) courtesy Springfield Armory NHS, US NPS (3); pp. 232-233: From top: (SPAR 3292) courtesy Springfield Armory NHS, US NPS; (PR.13071), (PR.8277), (PR.7700) ©Royal Armouries (3); pp. 234-235: Apic/ Getty Images; MPI/Getty Images; AFP/ Getty Images; Henry Grosinsky/Life Picture Collection/Getty Images; NBC Newswire/ Getty Images; AP; Bottom row: National Archives/Getty Images; Co Rentmeester/ Life Picture Collection/Getty Images; Ronald L. Haeberle/Life Picture Collection/Getty Images; Keystone-France/Getty Images; courtesy of TIME Inc.; p. 236: epp photos/ Newscom; p. 237: (PR.13352) ©Royal Armouries; p. 238: Henry Groskinsky/Life Picture Collection/Getty Images; George Frey/Getty Images; p.239: Glock: Yuri Arcurs/Getty Images; Film stills: Everett (4); pp. 240-241: Clockwise from top left: Joel Richards/Getty Images; (XXX.167) ©Royal Armouries; Corbis; courtesy of Steyr; pp. 242-243: Clockwise from top: (PR.12095), (PR.13964) ©Royal Armouries (2); zim246/Getty Images;(PR.2254) ©Royal Armouries; Corbis; pp. 244-245: Linnaeus Tripe/British Library/London/Bridgeman Images; p. 256: Larry Burrows/Time & Life Pictures

TIME
LIFE
BOOKS

Published by Liberty Street, an imprint of Time Inc. Books
225 Liberty Street
New York, New York 10281

LIBERTY STREET is a trademark of Time Inc.

Editorial director Stephen Koepp
Project editor Eileen Daspin
Art director Gary Stewart
Designer Ryan Moore
Editorial consultant Paul Barrett
Picture editor Crary Pullen
Reporter-researcher Mary Shaughnessy
Copy editor Joel Van Liew
Project manager Allyson Angle
Associate prepress manager Alex Voznesenskiy
Firearms consultant Cameron Hopkins
Special thanks to Elizabeth Austin, Allison Chi, Anne-Michelle Gallero, Rachel Hatch,
Christina Lieberman, Courtney Mifsud, Carol Pittard, Gina Scauzillo, Springfield
Armory, Royal Armouries, NRA Museums, Thomas Del Mar Ltd, Smithsonian
Institution

ISBN 10: 1-61893-365-5

ISBN 13: 978-1-61893-365-2

First edition, 2016

1 QGT 16

10 9 8 7 6 5 4 3 2 1

Time Inc. Books products may be purchased for business or promotional use. For
information on bulk purchases, please contact Christi Crowley in the Special Sales
Department at (845) 895-9858.

To order Time Inc. Books Collector's Editions, please call (800) 327-6388,
Monday through Friday, 7 a.m.-9 p.m., Central Time.

We welcome your comments and suggestions about Time Inc. Books.
Please write to us at:
Time Inc. Books

Attention: Book Editors

P.O. Box 62310
Tampa, Florida 33662-2310

timeincbooks.com